Backtrack
The voice behind music's greatest stars

Dedication

For Eduardo, who has seen the best and worst
of me and chooses both.

TESSA NILES

BACKTRACK

THE VOICE BEHIND MUSIC'S GREATEST STARS

BACKTRACK
The voice behind music's greatest stars

First published in 2015 by
Panoma Press Ltd
48 St Vincent Drive, St Albans, Herts, AL1 5SJ UK
info@panomapress.com
www.panomapress.com

Cover design by Michael Inns
Artwork by Karen Gladwell
Printed and bound in Great Britain by TJ International Ltd.

ISBN 978-1-909623-84-2

Contents

Acknowledgments

For their love and unshakable belief in me: my partner
Eduardo Mondlane Jr; my parents Leonard and Molly and
siblings Amanda and Ian Webb; Kate Ancketill, Janet and
Nyeleti Mondlane, Kristofer, Alessia, Mikaela and
Fallon Mondlane, Stella Webb and Pepi and Paul Knight.

Sincere thanks to Mindy Gibbins-Klein for getting me here
and to Michael Jackson for introducing us.

To my South African editor Hilary Phillips for her
invaluable work.

To Fiona Sanders-Reece for taking care of me all these years.

Heartfelt thanks also to Christien van Yzendoorn,
David Gemmel, Vicky Moore, Mart-Mari Lesch,
Sherilyn Jutronich, Natasha Goodall, Eftyhia Peroulis,
Christine Mouton, Anne Turner, Henrique Pinheiro, Rex and
Goodi Bloomstein, Gabrielle Vickery and Danielle Shirtcliff.

And to David Enthoven, Angelica Bergese, Brian Aris,
Marcus Vere, Anthony Critchlow, Valentine Johnson,
Jillie Bushell and Kemble Elliott.

Introduction

As the full force of the spotlights hit the stage, tiny beads of perspiration curled the stray hairs at the back of her neck. Stepping forward she tugged nervously at her dress, the net underskirt scratching at her bare legs. As his voice crackled over the tannoy, the compère dabbed at his glistening face. 'Ladies and gentlemen, please give a lovely warm Butlins welcome to... What's yer name, lass?' he hissed, staring blankly at the scribbles smudged on the napkin.

The girl bit sharply into her lip, certain that her heart was going to burst through her dress and splat on to the wooden floor beneath her feet. She'd practised the routine in her bedroom a thousand times – over and over again – and yet now couldn't even remember her own name.

Grabbing the young performer's trembling hand, the compère walked her forward to the centre of the stage and winked in a 'Go get 'em kid!' kind of way. Behind her, the musicians in the backing band dazzled in their gold lamé. Blinded by the glare of the footlights she could just make out the blurred edge of the stage and, beyond that, only the thickest blackness.

'Breathe girlie,' she whispered as the final bars of the introduction seemed to guide her with a magical force towards the microphone.

'Don't forget to e-nun-ci-ate darling, and don't forget to smile.'

Molly's words came to her as she reached out for the microphone stand. Grappling to adjust the height to her ten-year-old frame, she felt sick. With a final smoothing of her dress and one enormous breath the girl looked up, opened her mouth and sang...

CHAPTER ONE

From dog collars to diamanté

'Just sing this,' Ian barked as he repeatedly placed the needle on the Neil Sedaka record.

'Remember this part while I put a different one over the top of yours. Oi, Flossie, concentrate! Dad'll be home any minute, he'll kill us for playing around with his stuff.'

'But why can't I just do the tune?' I protested.

'Because it's too easy, anyone can sing the melody but not everyone can sing a harmony.'

And so it was, the harmonies and background vocals on records became way more fascinating than the lead singer's parts. I needed to understand the sound that was made as each individual voice sang a different melody and the incredible result when the different parts were sung together.

From as early as I can remember I'd worshipped the great singers: Stevie Wonder, The Carpenters, Ella Fitzgerald, The Jackson

Five and other giants from my elder sister's and parents' record collections. Their voices just grabbed me: The Carpenters with their lush, smooth arrangements and seemingly effortless harmonies; Stevie and his deeply soulful genius. I'd listen for hours to the records, dissecting each part of their complex vocals.

I began to hear the unique way singers built up layer upon layer with their voices, creating a silky smooth sound. My older brother Ian, who shared my passion, would constantly compete with me to find an extra harmony on a record, one that he and I felt the artist had somehow missed. It was nearly always a harmony that had been left out for good reason as the effect invariably sounded like a car horn by the time we'd finished.

Ian, Amanda, Tessa, Len and Molly Webb at Southend beach, 1964.

In 1966 my family moved from the town of Ilford to a four-bedroomed semi in the small suburb of Maidstone in Kent. The modest house overlooked an area of open land called Penenden Heath. In medieval times the heath had been a place of execution, where felons and suspected witches were hanged. In the 60s the only things found hanging were on my mother's washing line, and the gallows had been replaced by the local pub.

'I'M... NOT... GOING!' I spat.

With gritted teeth the five-year-old me wailed and clung like a demented monkey to my father's legs.

'You'll be fine, sweetheart, St Paul's is a lovely school and you'll soon make friends.'

My father winced as he tried with no success to prise my small but determined fingers from his thighs.

'Nooooo, Daddy, pleeeasse don't leave me here.'

Accustomed to the first-day reactions of young children, the kindergarten teacher crouched down beside me and whispered, 'Would you like to try on my shoes, they're brand new?'

With eyes wide I stared at Ruth Hughes. Her eyebrows were painted on in thin lines like two liquorish laces and she wore her jet black hair swept up at the back as if someone had hidden a bread roll underneath. Her lips and shoes were fire engine red and I was certain that she was the most beautiful person I'd ever seen.

After loosening the vice-like grip on my father I stared down at the shoes that Mrs Hughes had slipped off and pushed towards me. I was utterly smitten with this fabulous new person in my life and when, as a bonus, her red shoes made a satisfying clacking noise, I teetered off in them happily, without so much as a backwards glance at my relieved father.

Tessa, aged five, at St Paul's Primary School, Maidstone, 1966.

Ruth Hughes taught me how to read, write and play games, and from that first day at St Paul's she sparked my lifelong love of shoes. She had two sons, Clive and Paul. Clive worked as an entertainer at a Butlins holiday camp and Paul attended the same school as my brother, but a couple of years ahead of him. Paul Hughes and Ian became friends, teased girls and studied karate together. They both loved music and Paul, an exceptional pianist, was also a talented composer. At times Paul was brooding and frustrated at having no outlet for his musicality and he subsequently developed problems at school. He became a regular fixture at our house, often bunking school to drink afternoon tea and share his woes with my mother, Molly. She was kind and understood him.

1972 was the year of hot pants, long summer holidays and watching *Here Come the Double Deckers* on the family's newly acquired colour television. I roller-skated at the community centre to speakers blasting *Have You Seen Her?* by The Chi-Lites, and rode in the back of my dad's car as he drove my 17-year-old sister to the local Saturday night disco. Every second commercial on TV had a catchy sing-along jingle: the hard-to-forget one for R White's lemonade and the legendary *Just One Cornetto!* For Ian and me these ditties were just another opportunity to show off our vocal skills at full volume to anyone in the vicinity who would listen.

My big sister had a job. Six years older than me, to my mind Amanda was wildly sophisticated. The musical soundtrack to her teenage years was created by her heroes, David Bowie and The Temptations. Tall and skinny, Amanda looked model perfect in outfits designed by Ossie Clark and Biba, which she paired with sky-high platform shoes. More than anything I loved to wear my sister's shoes, although my feet were three sizes smaller than hers. This was only a problem until a friend and I discovered an ingenious solution.

'What are these for?' asked nine-year-old Jane Sugden as we dug through the multitude of underwear in the top drawer of Amanda's chest.

'Don't know, they look like those masks that doctors wear in an operating theatre,' I giggled, placing the two end loops of the curious looking white pads over my ears.

'No, silly, that's not right. My mum also has them and she's definitely not a doctor.'

'Well what do you think they're for then?'

'Maybe it's what the grown-ups use to keep their hair out of their faces, you know, when they're putting on make-up?' said Jane, demonstrating by placing the loops over each ear and sliding the rectangular pad over her dark hair.

A swift glance around the bedroom suddenly provided me with the only possible answer.

'I... know, I know,' I squealed. 'I absolutely know what they are. Give me four.'

Later that morning as Jane and I teetered off to the shops wearing Amanda's best platforms, I encountered my mother getting off the bus with her shopping. Molly took one look at us wearing my sister's shoes with the white pads clumsily stuffed into them and quickly ushered us the short distance back home, muttering something about 'monthlies and ladies' curses'.

When Amanda wasn't chasing me with a hockey stick for stealing her prized possessions, she did other grown-up stuff like dying her red hair blonde and buying new records almost every week. She was *so* cool. I wanted to be just like her when I grew up.

Four years older than me, my easy-going brother was a redhead like Amanda. Ian attended the local grammar school and was a promising footballer. He had so many freckles on his face he looked like he'd been sunburnt through a tea-strainer. Ian and I shared a love of music and on Sunday evenings he would record the Radio 1 chart show on his cassette player so that he and I could harmonise with the pop hits of the week. In spite of our easy relationship, he wasn't above a spot of teasing, however. When the neglect of my pet rabbit caused its untimely death, for a good six months after the tragedy he hissed 'murderer' at me at every opportunity.

The youngest in the family, at the age of 11 I was a complete tomboy. Mousey blonde hair, usually fashioned into straggly pigtails, added to my somewhat unkempt appearance and the consequence of still being a thumb-sucker was evident: I had protruding teeth. Little interested in boys, my 5p a week pocket money was mostly spent on listening closely to the music of any and every entertainer around me.

My parents, Len Webb and Molly Hardy, were introduced to each other at a cocktail party in the mid-1950s. At the time, my father was with his new wife, a young woman who died the following year of a brain tumour. Before they met at the party, my mother recalled travelling up to London by train one day seated opposite my father; she knew he was one of the Webb twins from a few streets away, but they had never been formally introduced. Molly remembered staring at him with admiration and thinking that he looked the kind of man she would like to marry. Luckily for me, in 1956 Molly and Len did marry. Both lovers of music, their record collection ranged from Bach to Tom Jones and from big band swing to songs from the musicals. Among Molly's favourites were *South Pacific*, *The Sound of Music* and *The King and I*. As a girl she had aspired to becoming a singer, but service in the army during World War II put paid to her dreams; by the late 1950s young women of her generation were encouraged to marry and build families instead of careers.

It's fair to say that music was everywhere and everything to me as I grew up. Ian and I sang in the local church choir and relished the 40p we'd receive for singing at weddings on Saturday afternoons. To relieve the interminable boredom of the ceremonies we devised a plan.

'Psst, Tess, did you bring it?' Ian mouthed from the opposite end of the choir pew.

'Yes… I did. Hang on.'

'C'mon quick, pass it along,' my impatient brother whispered as I carefully pulled up my starched white cassock and dug down into a lumpy white sock and pulled out a small foil-wrapped package.

The vicar in his sing-song voice began his sermon: 'Dearly beloved, we are gathered here in the sight of God and in the face of this company to join together this man and this woman…'

Checking to make sure that the congregation's eyes were fixed firmly on the bride and groom, I surreptitiously passed the package containing a large chunk of cheese along to my right. Each choir member carefully tore off a piece and passed it quickly along the pew.

Judging by the pinched expressions of the bride and groom's family in the front row pews, the aroma of cheese had wafted towards them.

'What the hell is this?' hissed the spotty boy next to me as he spat out the contents of his mouth into a copy of the order of service.

The vicar continued: 'Love is patient, love is kind, it is never envious or arrogant with pride...'

As his nose detected the powerful smell now invading the church, the vicar's eyes narrowed as he scanned the choir. His gaze landed firmly on me, who was red faced and guilty as original sin.

Later known by my fellow choristers as the 'stinky cheese incident' this little church mouse learned never ever to confuse cheddar with fully ripened and aged Stilton.

My fascination with all forms of entertainment grew. If taken to a show or Christmas pantomime I'd watch transfixed, carried away by a dream that one day I would be up there on stage. If there were children in the cast my emotions were akin to jealousy; I burned with the desire to change places. Desperate to follow my dreams of performing, I pleaded with my parents to let me go to a stage school, but it was not to be; Molly and Len insisted that I receive a formal education. Although never discussed, I knew that in reality my parents could never have raised the necessary fees.

As time went by the fixation of becoming a singer grew. Lack of interest in schoolwork and an obsession with achieving my dreams meant friendships with me were not for the faint-hearted; music entirely occupied my thoughts and deeds. Kim Harknett came from an upstanding family. She lived in a 70s townhouse and I was fascinated by her mum, a formidable woman who worked as a staff nurse in the local hospital but at home wore kaftans and smoked Consulate cigarettes. With her glossy brown hair and the longest eyelashes in Christendom, my friend Kim had many admirers. Her tendency to blush beetroot red at the slightest thing only added to her charm. But for me, Kim's most alluring quality was her taste in music. While other kids our age were listening to the Bay City Rollers and David Cassidy, we listened to the likes of Bread, Stevie Wonder, America and a little-known Scottish composer, Chris Rainbow. Pretty sophisticated taste for two spotty teenagers – kids who could also be found stealing apples, smoking cigarettes and sitting outside Ian's bedroom listening to him and Paul playing guitar.

'Oh God, he's soooo gorgeous,' mused a half-asleep Kim.

Lying on the less than plush landing carpet with our skinny legs up against the wall, we could hear the sounds of music coming from my brother's room.

'Eeurgh, no way, that's so weird,' I replied. 'Number one, he's old and besides Paul's too serious.'

'He's not that old, and I like that he's a bit, you know, a bit intense.'

'Well, you're on your own with that one, but he is really talented. He and Ian stay in that room for ever writing songs and whatever else it is they do, but my mum says that Paul's not doing very well at school.'

Suddenly the bedroom door burst open.

'Come in here you two,' said Ian registering the shock on both our faces.

'What, in there, with you?'

'Er, yeah, dingbat. Come on, Paul needs you to sing a harmony.'

I thought Kim was about to pass out as we carved a place to sit on the floor among the piles of clothes, dirty plates and school books.

I quickly picked up the part that Paul wanted me to sing. He sang the harmony to me a few times as he strummed on his guitar. The sound of my voice blending perfectly with the boys' lit a flame inside me. This was what I'd heard on all those records and had sung along with ever since I could remember, but now I was making that sound. It was easy for me. Right then and there I knew that this was the way to be truly happy in life, and I needed to find a way to make it happen.

Troubled Paul Hughes found himself expelled from Maidstone Boys' Grammar School and got a job as a hospital porter, working the night shift. With his new income, he and Ian set up a basic recording studio in a bedroom at Paul's parents' modest home. The boys wired in a 16-track tape recorder housed in a small control room and an assortment of microphones and headphones. As Paul began to coach me, I found every aspect of recording intriguing. With boundless patience he'd spend hours teaching me complicated harmonies, and I became obsessed with mastering them. The satisfaction of hearing my voice recorded over and over again (called tracking) seemed to me of far greater importance than anything learnt at school. Like my heroine, Karen Carpenter,

I created lush walls of voices and after school would run eagerly to record until it was dark outside. I'd then walk the short distance home, certain that under Paul's direction I was moving closer to my dream.

Keen to show off my skills to a wider audience, I pleaded with Paul to record a short version of me singing *Close To You* by The Carpenters. We entered it for the Capital Radio nationwide talent contest. Ian sent off the multi-tracked demo tape to the station and some weeks later, to my complete amazement, I received a telegram saying that I'd won first prize. At the time, the family was holidaying on a farm in Norfolk. There wasn't a pig, a cow or a sheep on that farm that didn't have the telegram waved under its nose. With my win as validation, I now saw no reason not to eat, sleep and breathe music.

Back at home almost every waking moment was spent working on my singing. The 'almost' part was filled in by my sudden and surprising interest in a boy. In actual fact he was more of a man. Peter drove a navy blue Triumph Spitfire and had a worldliness about him that boys my own age lacked. At 15½ I was ready to explore, but he was reticent about taking things further. Sometimes I'd bunk school and listen to stories of how his mother had hidden money behind the wallpaper in his living room. I was persuasive, and one night on his mother's living room floor I wore down his resolve. I never took my eyes off that wallpaper!

Paul signed a contract with a small publishing company that secured me a job singing in a recording studio after school, backing local artists. Other than the money I'd made in the choir at weddings, this was the first time I'd been paid to sing. The teenage kid in the school uniform felt as if she had the world at her feet. I couldn't believe how easy and natural it all felt. Attending school now seemed nothing but a hindrance to my driving ambition and as my passion for music grew, my schoolwork progressively worsened. At age 16, after a poor showing in my O Levels, I made the decision to release myself from the chains of academia forever.

During the summer of 1977, Queen Elizabeth's Silver Jubilee Year, punk rock reached its zenith. Punks, with their anarchic message and shocking appearance, provoked outrage among the establishment. Blessed with zero political leanings, no desire to see Margaret Thatcher ceremoniously ousted from power and no particular affinity with punk music, I focused on realising my dreams of stardom. For me, it was time to hit the road to the strains of *Chanson d'Amour* and *God Save the Queen*.

Hitting the road consisted of taking a summer job at the company where my father worked. HR Denne in Peckham, south London, was a family business that made uniforms for the Metropolitan Police Force. During week two I was promoted from the warehouse to a small factory upstairs where women from the East End made clerical collars for clergymen.

'Ere love, you wanna be careful with them poles. They'll burn ya,' laughed the middle-aged woman standing in front of me.

'Oh... right... erm, thank you very much,' I stammered as the lady turned to greet the reaction from her workmates who by now were all chuckling.

'Don't mind them, dear, they're just playing wiv ya. It's just that we don't get a lotta new girls in 'ere ya see. I'm Ivy, what's ya name love?'

'Er, Tessa. Tessa Webb.'

'Yeah we know. The boss's daughter, right?'

'Well, no, not exactly.'

'It's alright love, we don't bite, do we girls?' said a brassy blonde named Denise.

Denise, Ivy and the crew spent the summer teaching me how to cut out, press and mould the white plastic fabric around a heated pole to form the dog collars, singing along to the hits of yesteryear on Radio 2 as we worked. After a couple of weeks I was given the job of making clip-on ties, which had become an essential item of police uniform when too many coppers risked strangulation during criminal altercations. Throughout that summer I got to know and love the small team of women who worked on the factory floor: sisters from different sides of the track united by dog collars, Radio 2 and the warm smell of plastic.

The brief experience of working on a factory production line further fuelled my desire to chase my dream. Back home in Maidstone, Paul's older brother Clive had returned from his job entertaining British holidaymakers at a Butlins holiday camp. Clive, Paul and I began hatching plans to form a group. We needed another girl to complete the outfit. A friend passed on the contact details of Martin and Michelle Greene, a husband and wife who were both looking to work in music. After hearing Michelle sing we decided she should join us and Martin, her husband, became our manager. We named the group Sam. A wealthy property developer, Martin Greene was in the process of renovating a mansion in Cobham, a leafy suburban town in Surrey. Clive, Paul and his new wife Gail and I re-located to Silverwood, the mansion, and set up home in the annex of the main house. The empty drawing room at Silverwood became our rehearsal studio and, despite having to compete with the sound of builders' grinders and saws,

Sam – Part 1: Paul, Michelle, Tessa and David, 1978.

over the months our act began to take shape. The Hughes brothers had always had a volatile relationship, and living and working together began to re-open old issues between them; leadership struggles arose and tensions developed with Martin, the manager. At almost the end of our rehearsal period, during a highly explosive argument, Clive announced that working with Paul was untenable, packed his bags and left. Of all of us, Clive had the most experience and charisma.

Martin found us a replacement guitar player but now the tensions between Martin and Paul were growing. Paul and Gail then made the decision to leave. It was a bad moment: band members were dropping like flies and we hadn't yet done a gig. As I was still so young, Paul assumed I would return to Maidstone with Gail and himself, but even at the tender age of 17 it was crystal clear to me that he did not have the personality to make it. He had been my mentor, my friend and my tireless tutor, but after years of learning under his guidance I knew it was time for me to go it alone.

Michelle Greene, a wealthy Jewish girl, was what my father would call 'highly capable'. She rode horses, skied like an Olympian and knew everything there was to know about any kind of machinery. Once, when the fan belt of the car she was driving snapped, Michelle skilfully fashioned her tights into a workable replacement. Martin, who was considerably older than Michelle, adored everything about show business. He had inherited his wealth from his father's saccharine business and loved the idea of dabbling in show business.

After our short-lived exploits as a band, Michelle and I formed Sam, a cabaret duo. Together, we worked out songs and dance routines, and plundered the local markets for yards of lurex fabric and diamanté, which Michelle's mother made into revealing stage frocks. With the wave of a hairdresser's wand I underwent a transformation from mousey brown to beach blonde. At this point, the extent of my live performance experience was winning the talent show at Butlins. I could sing pretty much anything and my studio technique was good, but I had no performance skills and no clue how to entertain an audience. Michelle began teaching me how to present myself: how to put on stage make-up, dance in stilettos, pad my bra, use a microphone and apply blusher to highlight my rather small cleavage.

With my transformation complete, we set to work. Martin quickly found us an agent who got us jobs in nightclubs around the West End of London. If we were lucky we were able to use a dressing room, but most of the time we changed in the toilets that were shared with nightclub hostesses. Sam performed for ten minutes at a time and we would then rush to another club in the area to do the same routine, often working at two or three in one night. Despite the seediness of the clubs and the dubious nature of the clientele, I saw only the glamour; the thrill of audience response and applause stirred my soul. This was where I needed to be, and with my new-found confidence I felt unstoppable.

One evening a fellow cabaret performer, Diana Darvey, and I chatted post-show. Sitting in the store cupboard doubling as a make-shift dressing room where we carefully packed away feathers, sequined dresses and make-up, Diana regaled me with stories of her days as the favourite muse of one of Britain's best loved TV personalities. She had risen to fame on *The Benny Hill Show* with her stunning performances and gravity-defying outfits.

'Darling girl, I've been having a think,' said Diana guiding a stray hair behind her ear with a perfectly polished fingernail. 'My friend Benny is casting girls for his new TV series and I think you ought to go and try out.'

It took a moment to register her suggestion. 'You're joking, right? I should just call up *the* Benny Hill out of the blue?' I said in disbelief.

An unforgiving neon light flickered above our heads as Diana proceeded to pull a pen and paper from her handbag and scribbled down a phone number. Handing me the piece of paper she said, 'Tell him you're a friend of Diana Darvey and that I said you're great.'

She fixed me with a heavily lashed stare and continued.

'Listen to me, there's no time for shyness in showbiz, my darling, you've just gotta do it. You've got the talent, now go out there and sell yourself.'

An icon of British light entertainment, Benny Hill had delighted audiences around the world for years with his popular brand of sexual innuendo and slapstick. The next day, without a second thought or hint of nerves, I dialled the number.

'Hello?'

'Oh, hello... erm... is this Benny? I've been given your number by Diana Darvey who said that you might be looking for girls to audition.'

'Yes,' said the voice calmly. 'You do have the right number. Now tell me, dear, what exactly is it you do?'

I proceeded to rattle off the reasons why he absolutely had to meet Michelle and me. Contrary to public perception of him as a lascivious sexist, Benny was charming and gracious on the phone. He explained that he was not really looking for singers but that Sam should come up to London to meet him as he was holding auditions for his new television series.

Covent Garden, the dance capital of England, sizzled on that scorching July day. Decked out in full make-up, matching satin catsuits and gold heels, Michelle and I tottered up Long Acre towards the Pineapple Dance Studios. For some inexplicable reason I'd donned a long curly wig for the audition and was already sweating profusely under it. When you commit to wearing a wig there is no turning back as one's own hair becomes a matted, soupy mess underneath.

At the studio Michelle and I joined hundreds of other hopefuls in the corridors who, like us, were waiting to peddle their wares.

As we watched the oh-so-limber dancers warming up it began to dawn on us that perhaps this might have been a mistake.

'Micho,' I whispered nervously. 'What the hell are we doing here? These girls are all serious dancers.'

'Stop panicking, we're here now and we're not that bad, let's just go for it,' said an unconvincing Michelle. 'Just copy what the others are doing and we'll be alright.'

Groups of 15 girls at a time were ushered into the main dance studio, where Benny Hill sat quietly in the corner. Music blared out of a ghetto-blaster on to the busy streets below while the choreographer taught everyone the routine. The dancers strutted and kicked their way through the elimination process until the minuscule choreographer decided on three or four 'possibles' from each group.

When our names were called, Michelle and I placed ourselves strategically at the back of the group, who were resplendent in Lycra and leg warmers. Even with the windows open the air inside the studio was stifling. With no fans we were sweltering even before dancing a step. Surprisingly, Michelle, who had far more dance experience than I had, was dismissed after the very first run-through. Continuing to skulk at the back of the group, I kept my head down and did my best to act invisible – a difficult job with mirrors revealing you from every wall of the studio. With each run-through the group thinned out until, by some fluke, I found myself among the last four dancers. I was now sweating so profusely that the dark sweat marks on my catsuit expanded by the minute and I had to keep surreptitiously adjusting my wig, which was shifting position. With no one left in the line-up to hide behind, it was suddenly me and three others at the front. As the music fired up for the final time I whispered my trusty mantra,

'Breathe girlie.'

Hoarse by now, the choreographer shouted, '*And* a-one, two, three and spin two three and kick... those... legs...'

By some act of God I had the moves down at this point and proceeded to throw myself around the studio with the zealousness of the convert. From working with Michelle I knew that the ending of any routine needed to be impressive, so as the final bars approached I thrust up my hand dramatically, punched the air and threw my head back with a flourish.

'Hold it... hold the pose,' screamed the choreographer.

Gasping for breath I held the pose alright but, sadly, the inanimate object on my head had other plans. The now sweat-drenched wig slithered off my head and plopped like a damp sponge on to the floor behind me. I spun round and scooped up the sorry mess to the sound of Benny Hill howling with laughter.

'Brilliant, absolutely brilliant,' he roared.

Although mortified, I could see the absurdity of the situation and joined in. Benny walked across the dance studio, hugged me warmly and thanked me for the enjoyable performance. It came as no surprise when Michelle and I did not pass the dance audition, but I had the honour of humouring the late great comedian himself, Mr Benny Hill.

With the assistance of a newly procured agent, Sam was introduced to Derek Agutter, a former army officer and the entertainment organiser for Combined Service Entertainment (CSE), the official provider of live entertainment to the British armed forces. Derek was the father of the actress Jenny Agutter. Through him, Sam was sent as part of a concert party to entertain the British

Sam – Part 2: Michelle and Tessa (in that wig), 1979.

troops in Northern Ireland. At the height of the troubles there Michelle and I, in our risqué outfits, provided a much-needed morale boost to the British boys in uniform. Why we were never honoured with a knighthood or at least a medal I shall never know, for at times we were genuinely terrified. The city of Belfast, with its bombed-out buildings and the Crumlin Road barracks, was as close to a war zone as one could imagine. While travelling through the depressed streets in armoured vehicles, our merry band of CSE entertainers was regularly ordered to 'hit the floor' when the security escorts spotted snipers in the bushes. After our fifth tour of duty in Northern Ireland Michelle and I decided to hang up our flak jackets and combat heels for good, and find work that would involve significantly less danger.

In stark contrast to our previous posting, Sam's next engagement was a six-week residency at an elegant hotel on the beautiful island of Madeira. Not a soldier was in sight as Michelle and I entertained the diners at The Savoy for 40 minutes, five nights a week. The cream of British session musicians was in the backing band (not that, at the time, I really knew what a session player did). The musicians, who were taking a break from their regular studio work in London, regarded the hotel job as a paid holiday.

When I heard the calibre of their playing I was astounded. I'd never heard musicians play like that before. Their standard of musicianship was on an entirely new level and I discovered that they too loved the music that I had grown up listening to. We were kindred spirits and I spent as much time as I could hanging out with them, listening to them jamming together and enthralled by their stories about life in London's session world. It all sounded so impressive. These guys hired out their services to record producers and composers for a minimum of three hours at a time, and charged a fee. Once again, I began to sense that a change was coming. Working with Michelle had been fun, but instinctively I knew that I had to keep moving forward; that if I looked hard enough something challenging was just round the corner. When the Madeira engagement ended I exchanged numbers with the band members and received an open invitation from them to meet up on our return to the UK. For me, seeing them again couldn't come soon enough.

At the start of the 1980s Michelle and I auditioned for a new BBC talent show called *Search for a Star*. Sam was featured in the *Radio Times* magazine, the BBC's weekly guide to what was on television, a copy of which was in virtually every household in the country. It's difficult to imagine now, but in those days there were only three TV channels in Britain. As the prime time TV entertainment on Saturday nights, *Search for a Star* offered massive exposure. With the whole of Britain tuned in to watch, we had a strong feeling that this was going to be our time to shine.

With the help of a hired musical director who endeavoured to make Sam less cabaret and more contemporary in style, we made it through to the competition finals. Among the seven other finalists, Sam was competing against a child performer and a ventriloquist with a talking duck. Michelle and I were quietly confident that our performance would decimate the competition, but despite the flowers sent to our dressing room, the bottles of champagne and telegrams of support, nothing was able to alter our destiny that fateful Saturday night. After a lukewarm reception, poor Sam suffered a crushing defeat: we were beaten into the second-last place by a ventriloquist's duck and a flippin' kid!

It was time to move on. Working with Sam had been an invaluable experience, and with Michelle's help I'd gained confidence and experience as a performer. The Greenes had always been generous and supportive, but my future now lay elsewhere. During the ill-fated talent show our musical director, Alan Townsend, mentioned that he'd like me to meet friends of his who were looking for a singer. Still living at Silverwood and very much under the wing of the Greenes, I knew that I needed to make plans to go it alone and cast my fate to the wind. While deciding what move to make next I contacted Dill Katz, the bass player from the fabulous backing band I'd met in Madeira. I arranged to meet Dill in London to sit in on a recording session he was working on for an artist called Sarah Brightman. Sarah had recently split from her group, Hot Gossip, and was in the process of launching a solo career.

The small but perfectly formed Radio Luxemburg studios were tucked discreetly behind the Hilton Hotel on Park Lane. Having worked in local studios as a youngster I was familiar with the set-up, but this professional studio was in another league. Dill introduced me to the engineer and the producer of the session, Richard Niles, a slightly built 28-year-old with an American accent. Dressed in a Fair Isle sweater, corduroy trousers, and wearing quirky horn-rimmed glasses, the pages of his musical score were scattered across the mixing desk. Richard was welcoming and funny in a Woody Allen kind of way. As he skilfully directed them, between takes he and the musicians engaged in hilarious banter. I was immediately attracted to him.

I was in awe of the musicians, who played effortlessly and repeatedly until Richard was satisfied that he had the track he needed. Listening to the playing and camaraderie of these people further enforced my passion for the studio environment. I loved the accuracy that could be achieved during the recording process. In a live situation you had only one shot at getting it right, but in the studio it was possible to achieve perfection. I knew this was exactly the environment I needed to be in.

'OK guys, it's a wrap,' announced Richard in his LA twang. 'Great work everyone, who's up for drinks next door?'

Trader Vic's was located in the basement of the Hilton Hotel. The restaurant, decked out in Tiki style with Polynesian artefacts and potted palms, seemed an exotic location as Richard and I chatted comfortably. He was smart and I was drawn to his humour. Sipping on my very first Piña Colada, thankful to be catching up with my musician pals, it was clear to all that I really had eyes for only one man.

Back at Silverwood, Alan Townsend was planning to introduce me to three friends of his who were successfully working the international cabaret circuit and looking to secure a recording contract. Valentine Johnson, Jillie Bushell and Theresa Wood went under the fantastically camp name of The Shades of Love and were looking for a fourth member to join them. Alan arranged for me to meet up with the group at a Chrysalis record company party at a warehouse in Chelsea. My outfit of choice, designed to impress, was a purple silk shirt paired with shocking pink spandex trousers and, of course, killer heels. The group members were super-friendly and at the earliest opportunity suggested we all take a spin on the dance floor – a ruse on their part to check out my moves. Alan had vouched in no uncertain terms for my vocal abilities, so it was really down to whether my personality was the right fit for them and whether or not I had two left feet.

Sensing that this was actually my audition I managed not to embarrass myself on the dance floor, and after a brief discussion with Valentine, the girls informed me that I was in! I learned that we would be off to Dubai in two weeks' time on a six-week contract, performing in a small hotel for one hour a night. With costumes to buy, contracts to sign and an entire show to learn in double-quick time, I set to work. Upon our return from Dubai the group would be going into the studio to record songs for a possible recording deal. Deliriously happy, I buzzed with excitement at the thought of this new adventure, at being one quarter of The Shades of Love. Val, Jill, Terry and I were then ushered through the party to meet – of all people – Sarah Brightman who, to my complete surprise, was accompanied for the evening by the intriguing American producer, Richard Niles.

CHAPTER TWO

We three Stings

Val, Jillie, Terry and I sealed our new arrangement with champagne and I spent the rest of the evening chatting to Richard Niles, who was witty, well read and highly entertaining. Despite years of living in England his American accent was undiluted and he told me how, aged 11, he'd moved from America to Britain with his mother, Pat, and stepfather, Jesse, who were both authors. Fascinating and worldly, Richard was obviously interested in me and though clearly a little star-struck I was shocked at how much I liked him.

We arranged to meet up again soon, but two weeks after the party, with songs learnt, routines polished and stage outfits fitted, I was ready to embark on the six-week contract in Dubai. When I told Molly where I was going to work she feared I'd be sold into white slavery, never to be seen again. In 1980 Dubai was not the thriving metropolis we know it as today. However, always supportive, despite their reservations my parents wished me luck. Richard and I became close very quickly and my fledgling relationship with him was barely off the ground when I departed for the Dubai gig; we both wondered if our relationship would survive this potential derailment.

In a difficult conversation with Martin and Michelle I told them that I would be moving on; although both were saddened at my decision they graciously let me know they understood. With a heavy heart I packed my bags, nervous at the idea of leaving them and Richard for the uncharted territory of the Arab emirate.

'Oh my God, could it get any hotter?' I puffed as Val, Jilly, Terry and I piled into the air-conditioned taxi outside Dubai airport.

'Welcome to the UAE, dear Tess. You'd better be careful or you'll burn to a crisp out here in minutes,' advised Val. 'The Dubai Marine Hotel please, driver, and can you crank up that fan?'

'Will I need to be careful of anything else here? I know nothing about the culture,' I asked nervously as the car rattled along.

'Well,' said Jilly, 'just be respectful with your dress and don't accept any gifts from anyone after the show otherwise we may never get you home.'

'Gee thanks, Jill, that makes me feel great.'

Downtown Dubai consisted of a cluster of office buildings, a handful of hotels and a great deal of sand. Speeding through the dusty streets and across the city's creek which was once the centre of Dubai's pearl trade and still bobbing with ancient dhows, the sun glinted from the minarets and the sounds of the Imams' call to prayers could be heard all around. Once settled into our hotel, the remainder of the day was spent acclimatising and rehearsing for the show. Life soon settled into a flow. Rehearsals in the mornings and in the afternoons we'd escape the sweltering city in a borrowed jeep and head for the beach. Sometimes we'd trawl the gold souks for bargains, bartering with the shop-keepers. At night, we'd perform the show and then it was time to party. This was indeed the life! Working as part of a team was a joy: Valentine was a skilled showman, Jillie a charismatic force on stage and Terry the band's elfin-faced flower child, with a back-ground in West End shows. She and I shared a room, her side neatly decorated with driftwood, postcards and art work, while mine was piled high with clothes and mess. Terry was patient and learned to be tolerant of my chaos.

The Shades of Love: Jillie, Valentine, Tessa and Terry, 1979.

Our nightly shows soon became polished and slick and I was given great solos to sing. One of them was a challenging Stevie Wonder song called *All in Love Is Fair*. Not your typical cabaret number at all as Valentine, who was also our musical director, insisted we performed classic material. Our residency at the Dubai Marine Hotel was a hit and upon our return to England we went straight into a local studio to work on a couple of new songs. The group secured a recording contract with Magnet Records and was booked into RAK studios to record a single and B side. The A side was a cover version of Smokey Robinson's *You Really Got a Hold on Me*. It felt amazing to be back in the studio, my spiritual home. The band's name was changed to Chance, which was only marginally better than The Shades of Love.

My relationship with Richard Niles progressed quickly and I spent more and more time at his apartment. After only a few weeks he asked me to move in with him, and I moved my last few belongings from Silverwood to his comfortable one-bedroomed flat in Swiss Cottage.

Richard introduced me to his mother, Pat, who had been an acting starlet in 1940s Hollywood. She had married Richard's father, a troubadour of Italian descent by the name of Tony Romano; they had two children together, Lisa and Richard, but the marriage was short-lived and Pat and Tony parted in an acrimonious divorce. Pat then married Jesse Lasky Junior, the son of Paramount Pictures mogul, Jesse Lasky. An author, successful screenwriter and member of Hollywood movie royalty, Jesse Junior had written the screenplays for Cecil B DeMille movie epics such as *The Ten Commandments* and *Samson and Delilah*.

Pat, Jesse and 11-year-old Richard moved from Hollywood to London in the swinging 60s. Richard's sister, Lisa, remained in California with their father. A studious child, he longed to play

*Richard Niles
and Tessa, 1981.*

an instrument like his father, but was forbidden to by Pat as she did not want her son to take the same musical path. Pat and Jesse wrote scripts for *The Saint* and other popular British TV series of the time, and were part of the 1960s London social scene. Richard recalled how once, while he lay in bed proofreading one of his parents' scripts, Ringo Starr poked his head round the bedroom door and said hello. The young Richard remembered the indignity he had felt at being caught in his pyjamas by a member of The Beatles.

Educated at The American School in London, Richard eventually resorted to smuggling a guitar into his parents' apartment and kept it hidden under his bed. For some time he managed to hide his musical dreams from his mother, but his secret was eventually revealed as his talent was so evident that even Pat could no longer deny it. Richard then went to study at the Berklee College of Music in Boston, where he said he 'majored in Composition, Counterpoint and Sarcasm'. After returning to England he began working as an arranger for his long-time friend and fellow-American, the producer Steve Rowland.

At 29, Richard was ten years older than me and many people saw Svengali-like traits in him when it came to our relationship. From the very beginning he made it clear that I needed to stop working the cabaret circuit and concentrate on honing my vocal skills in London. He felt building my reputation among studio musicians was crucial, and being in love with him, I was more than happy to follow his roadmap. Taking instruction from one of the most highly respected musicians in London seemed absolutely the right thing to do.

Richard introduced me to established players on the session scene and I began to receive offers of work. Mitch Dalton, a guitarist who was himself in great demand, recommended me for a job in a function band that played at weddings and bar mitzvahs.

'It's an easy gig, Tess, you just have to know the tunes in the Top 20 and a few classics,' Mitch confided. 'It'll be a doddle and I think you'll really enjoy it. But I do think maybe I should warn you about the other girl you'll be singing with.'

I must have looked concerned as Mitch continued, 'Her name's Pepi Lemer and some people find her a bit... difficult.'

As it happened Mitch was right, I did find her difficult – difficult not to like! I was the new girl on the job who knew next to nothing about being in a function band and Pepi guided me selflessly and humorously through it. She was warm, funny and friendly and I couldn't fathom what Mitch was thinking when he warned me about her. I could see immediately that she had a strong personality but in my opinion that could only be a plus. We were from radically different backgrounds and not close in age, but in no time at all forged a strong bond. Friendships like that don't happen too often and we've always wondered why we were so drawn to each other. Over the years we have sustained our deep affection, and our friendship, peppered with laughter and tears, has weathered the trials and tribulations of our lives.

At this point Richard and I began writing songs together and if the opportunity arose he would recommend me to sing on projects that he was working on. I managed always to impress as my voice was well-suited to studio work, but I knew only too well that the real challenge would be to prove myself over and above being the producer's girlfriend.

In my newly acquired Fiat Panda, blasting The Human League's *Don't You Want me Baby?* I thought I was quite the thing about town. It was 1981 and London was pulsing to the sounds of electronic music. Richard and his mother had convinced me to see an orthodontist about my protruding teeth, a consequence of my thumb-sucking days. I had been a major thumb-sucker as a kid and loath as I was to admit it, the teeth did need fixing. It was a challenge learning how to sing with a mass of wire in my mouth, especially when I was booked for a radio commercial for the Meat Marketing Board. I had enormous difficulty getting my lips around the phrase 'Cooking with stewing steak' which I managed to make sound like 'Cooking with sschtooing sschteak'.

In between tours with the Shades of Love, my new best friend Pepi and I continued to have way too much fun singing together on the wedding and bar mitzvah circuit. As the only non-Jew in the band I was given the honour of singing the Yiddish songs, my favourite being *Bei Mir Bist Du Shein*. Some of the scenarios we found ourselves in on gigs were unbelievable. Pepi had a wicked sense of humour and she and I needed no encouragement in the laughter department; at times, the pressure of having to remain professional posed a serious challenge for both of us. On one occasion the 93-year-old grandmother of the bar mitzvah boy was wheeled into the function room in her hospital bed, complete with drip, and pushed around the dance floor by a nurse to the strains of *The Hokey Cokey*. Rendered completely incapacitated at the sight, Pepi and I collapsed in uncontrollable laughter, unable to continue singing. The furious bandleader threatened to fire us if we didn't pull ourselves together immediately. He threatened that a lot.

With new work opportunities beginning to bear fruit in London it became time to say goodbye to Valentine, Jillie and Terry. They too had become my great friends but our attempts at

Pepi Lemer, 1980

changing direction with the recording deal hadn't worked out, so I announced my intention to leave the group. Today, Val is still tearing it up on the function circuit, Jillie runs her own successful agency, booking talent, and Terry lives in Ibiza running a T-shirt business. As always, it was hard to say goodbye to people with whom I'd formed a close bond, but under Richard's guidance my career was moving quickly forward and my own unstoppable ambition proved to be a powerful motivator.

Morrissey Mullen was a jazz fusion group firmly established on the London pub scene. Dick Morrissey played sax and Jim Mullen played guitar with a unique hammering style. Their band, a six-piece, had a large following and was looking for a new singer. They asked me to join them and we worked three or four nights a week. At the regular Tuesday night gig at the Half Moon pub in Putney the crowd were so tightly packed into the room at the rear of the pub that I sometimes feared for their safety. Dick and Jim being masterful musicians, the gigs were fantastic. Paid solely in cash, throughout a year of working with Morrissey Mullen I never once needed to go to the bank.

Through Richard, I was introduced to many extraordinary musicians. One of them was a young jazz funkateer by the name of Jean-Paul Maunick, the founder of a band called Incognito. The band was looking for a singer and we recorded tracks that, though unsuccessful commercially, helped to further establish me on the all-important session scene.

In January 1982 I received a call for a studio job in London's East End. On arriving there I was met by the sound engineer, Gary Langan, who introduced me to a skinny, rag-tail group of musicians named ABC. The tall, tufty-haired lead singer's name

Incognito, a Tessa and Jean-Paul Maunick publicity shot
for their 1981 single.

was Martin Fry. Gary then introduced me to the producer of the session, who was wearing the biggest white rimmed glasses I had ever seen. In his soft northern accent he told me his name was Trevor Horn. Listening to the tracks I was immediately struck by innovative electronic sounds I'd not heard used before: synthesized and sampled sounds merged with lush strings that were cleverly fused with Martin's voice in lyrics that spoke of heartache and unrequited love. This sound was something really different. I sang lead and backing vocals on a track called *Date Stamp*. Under Trevor's direction I achieved what he wanted to hear and was happy that I'd been able to show off my skills to him. Little did I know that this experience would fast-track me into the session scene and place me firmly on the London music map.

Richard and I were becoming rising stars. He was achieving success as an arranger and producer, and I was working full-time, proving myself as a professional and accurate singer for live gigs and in the studio. One evening after supper at his parents' apartment, Richard proposed to me. Together we made a strong musical partnership and I saw no reason not to say yes to his marriage proposal. The truth was, though, that I didn't take the time to think it through and stifled any feelings that this might not be the best plan. We were a good team and life was going well; there seemed to be no real reason not to go ahead. With any doubts pushed firmly out of my mind, Richard and I set a date for the wedding, 9 February 1982.

Hurtling down the road towards the Marylebone registry office in my car that cold February morning, Pepi turned to me.

'Tessie? Can I ask you a serious question? Look, I know my timing sucks but I have to ask you this or I'll never forgive myself. Are you absolutely sure you're doing the right thing?' I took my eyes off the road long enough to see the worry etched on her face and knew already of her concerns.

'Yes, driving myself to my own wedding is a little unconventional I admit but hey, that's just me being a crazy chick, right?'

'Boobala, don't joke, you know what I mean. Are you doing the right thing marrying Richard?'

With my antique wedding dress and borrowed fox fur jacket from Pepi's vintage-rich wardrobe, I quite fancied myself as Daisy Buchanan from *The Great Gatsby*, though I doubted she would be seen in anything less than a Silver Ghost.

'Of course it's the right thing,' I said, my eyes fixed firmly ahead. 'And anyway if it turns out to not be the right thing then that would be OK too. God… cheer up. Life's too short to worry about these things. It'll be fine, don't worry.'

The expression of concern on Pepi's face told me that this was not the reassurance she was looking for and certainly not the best way for her closest friend to enter married life…

With Richard at the helm, Morrissey Mullen went into the studio to record the album *It's About Time*. For me, the transition from gigs to the studio was comfortable as we'd worked together live for many months. Though released to good reviews, the album failed to set the world alight. Meanwhile ABC's debut album, *The Lexicon of Love*, was setting the world alight. Released in 1982, it swiftly reached number one in the British charts and Trevor Horn and the team on the album became the 'must have' musicians in the industry. However, although the album sat in the number one position for several weeks, and despite several reminders, I had not received the £100 payment due to me from the record company, so with all the zealousness of youth I marched into the ABC record company's reception and demanded that I be paid, stating that I would not leave the offices until I was. After 30 minutes a rather embarrassed-looking receptionist handed me a cheque for £100. Undoubtedly I was also gaining confidence in handling the business side of my career. I was on a number one record and not afraid to make this point!

'Can you get to the John Henry rehearsal rooms by 4 o'clock this afternoon?' barked an unfamiliar voice down the phone. 'It's an audition for a US tour with a well-known band. The tour starts in five days. Can't tell you who it is yet, sorry.'

'Oh OK… great, would you mind hanging on for one minute, I just need to check my diary,' I lied, rifling through papers in an attempt to sound as if I had a frantic schedule.

'Erm, actually, yes, yes, I believe I can make it, what's the address?'

Changing into my best ripped jeans and stripy shirt, I jumped into a black cab to the popular north London rehearsal venue. With no one to greet me, no introduction and enormous trepidation I heaved open the giant steel door of the studio. Inside, Sting, Andy Summers and Stewart Copeland were in full musical flight, powering their way through *Can't Stand Losing You*, a magnificent sound barely contained by the normally adequate soundproofing. At the end of the song, with my heart pounding and the final chord still ringing in my ears, I walked across the room and introduced myself to the three members of The Police.

At 22 years old I had never before encountered a bona fide rock star, let alone three of them. Sting looked achingly handsome in T-shirt and combat trousers, his hair dyed red after having just filmed his role in David Lynch's *Dune*. With no idea what I was supposed to do next, I waited.

'I think you should come to my house tomorrow for a bit of a sing-song. Can you find your way to Hampstead alright?'

'And do you know any other singers with American passports because we leave for the US in five days and don't have enough time to apply for them?'

Oh dear God, now I had to speak. To Sting.

'Yes, I can come to Hampstead and I can ask an American friend of mine to come too.'

My smile was far too fixed for such a mundane statement but I was just so nervous.

'Right then,' said Sting, 'that's settled. See you tomorrow.'

The following day, me the one Brit and two Americans stood around the grand piano in Sting's living room in genteel Hampstead. *Every Breath You Take* was at number one around the world, and as we routined the vocals I felt the need to say something.

'I really like the way you have the backing vocals sounding country-esque in the bridge section.'

Sting stopped playing abruptly and gave me a withering look worthy of immediate dismissal.

'What exactly do you mean by that?' he said coldly, his eyes narrowed.

Holy crap, I'd really said the wrong thing. He was clearly miffed at having his vocals likened to anything resembling country music.

My attempt to diffuse the tension was blundering.

'I just mean that the voicing of the harmonies reminds me of that style of music... I didn't mean to...'

Too intimidated to say anything, the other singers clearly would have liked to have hidden under the piano. The silence was beyond uncomfortable and just as I was about to utter an apology Sting threw back his gorgeous head and laughed – a deep, throaty cackle of a laugh.

'That's just my Geordie humour comin' out pet. Don't mind me. Let's finish the song so we can move on. We've all got a tour to do.'

With the three singers hired, The Police went straight into full production rehearsal. With so many songs to learn and almost no time to learn them, Ray Schell, Shady Calver and I needed to pick up serious speed in order to prepare for the tour. We were expected to be able to listen to the original tracks and work out the vocal parts without instruction, a skill that was to serve me well throughout my career. Sting was having problems with his voice and the singers were hired with a view to taking some of the vocal strain off him, as singing lead vocals with his intensity required serious vocal stamina. Touring is an extreme test for any vocalist, so with our support Sting could rely on the background singers to carry some of the weight, although in reality he seldom did. Ray, Shady and I were instructed to sing with no vibrato and at full power all the time.

Vibrato is described as 'a musical effect consisting of a regular pulsating change of pitch, used to add expression to vocals'. Once one has learned to sing with vibrato it's extremely difficult to sing without it, especially in a live situation and when singing in unison with others. I've always found that apart from helping with tuning it also protects the voice from strain. However, the requirement for us was to be three Stings, getting as close as we could to his sound. So three Stings we became. The few days we had before our departure for the US tour were packed frantically with practice and more practice. The set list had not yet been decided upon, so we three Stings familiarised ourselves with every Police song ever written.

Our stage clothes were being made by a designer from a prestigious English theatre company. With our expectations high, Ray, Shady and I imagined ourselves in sexy little numbers and were shocked beyond belief when we finally saw what had been cho-

Tessa and Shady Calver in their 'shrouds', The Police Tour, 1983

sen. We could not possibly have imagined that on a high-profile tour with the most successful band in the world we were expected to wear voluminous black shrouds. And to complete the look we were given yashmaks, the veils worn by Muslim women so that only the eyes are exposed to public view. A puzzling choice, it was also pretty devastating as there was no way at all we singers would be seen by an audience. But with no time to protest I said my farewells to Richard and boarded the flight to the United States, embarking on the biggest adventure of my life.

The Synchronicity tour of 1983 kicked off in Illinois. Chicago was hot and humid, but not even the scorching temperatures could compare with the baptism of fire I was about to receive. A touring virgin, I was unprepared for life on the road. Everything – and I mean everything – was done to excess: the huge stadium gigs; the private jets and helicopters; the luxury hotels, houses and limousines; the police escorts. There were spas in Texas and skiing trips in Colorado, ball games in Biloxi and, of course, the nightly parties. Though readily available and widely used by many on the tour, drugs were really not my thing; I tried them on a couple of occasions but never felt the effect enough to want to continue. I also had no tolerance for alcohol, which I guess was surprising as most people around me were snorting or smoking or drinking something. Suffice it to say that a rock 'n' roll tour is an overwhelming phenomenon for a 22-year-old experiencing it for the first time.

The stadiums held from 12,000 to 30,000 people, and the noise of the crowds deafened at every show. Pre-show, the atmosphere in the stadium and backstage was electric. Security guards, caterers, arena staff and management, roadies, wives and girlfriends added to the growing excitement. In his dressing room, Sting's muscles took a pummelling from the strong hands of a masseur. Sting would then suspend himself by his feet from a contraption that looked remarkably like an instrument of torture, and simply hang. Shyness prevented me from asking why. The drummer, Stewart, and his faithful roadie, Jeff Seitz, strapped up his hands with tape to protect them from the painful effects of his adrenalin-fuelled performances. Closer to show-time the number of people in the dressing rooms thinned to a few. This was now the inner sanctum where the performers could focus on the task ahead. For the next two hours the six of us would belong to the audience. As the show blasted off, the crowd literally went insane. Sting tore across the stage powered by Stewart's frenetic

Sting backstage on The Police Tour, 1983.

back beat, while Andy's trademark arpeggios rang out around the stadium. As The Police thundered through hit after hit, their blonde heads flashed up on the massive video screens.

The first shows were unlike anything I had ever experienced before. Nothing could have prepared me for performing to thousands upon thousands of people. The heady mix of music and success was intoxicating. Still struggling with our outfits, Ray, Shady and I tried wearing the yashmaks but, not surprisingly, the material got caught in our mouths and it became impossible to sing. Thankfully, we were allowed to ditch the yashmaks but the shapeless tents remained. During outdoor shows the wind blew up inside them, giving us the appearance of three huge black blimps. Not pretty, and definitely not sexy. When the Synchronicity tour reached the east coast of America, instead of staying in hotels the band set up a base in a mansion in the town of Bridge Hampton, New York. On show days we'd fly in our private jet from Bridge Hampton to the venue and then fly back again after each performance.

The tour continued its furious pace, but I was not at all happy with the backing vocal sound. Ray and Shady had excellent voices but being a good backing vocalist requires a very different skill from singing lead. Background vocals require you to be able to blend your voice with whomever you are singing. The ability of backing singers to merge their voices together in a smooth sound is crucial. It's absolutely not about standing out or showing off your individual sound; it's about teamwork and creating a sound that fully supports the artist you're working with. This was not happening, particularly when we sang in unison together. The fact that we were not able to use vibrato was also proving to be really difficult. Our tuning was off, and at times so bad that Kim Turner, the out-front sound engineer, told me that he would turn the other singers down in the mix. I'd listen to tapes of the show and cringe. It really wasn't working, and believing in the old adage 'you're only as good as your weakest link', I began to fear for my job.

I did not know it, but Sting was working on finding replacements for the other two backing singers and asked if I would help him audition two ladies who had been highly recommended. Dolette McDonald and Michelle Cobbs, both seasoned professionals, were invited to audition when the band reached Los Angeles. Sting hid behind the door of the rehearsal room and listened as I taught the applicants their parts. What a sound we made together! These singers knew their stuff and were experienced vocalists. Both had come from a gospel background and knew exactly how to blend their voices as part of a group. Dolette and Michelle were hired, and Shady and Ray returned to England and individual success: Shady as a solo singer in Iceland and Ray as an actor, author, director and producer.

Dolette McDonald and I became instant friends. A New Yorker, she exuded confidence and the kind of worldliness I could only aspire to. Her hair was fashioned into fine dreadlocks and she was entirely comfortable in her enviable skin. Dolette's fashion sense was acute, but in answer to wardrobe enquires she'd simply say, 'Oh honey, just put a belt on it and call it a day.'

Hilariously funny, she could also be outrageous, the first time being when she was shown the stage outfits.

'Oh hell no!' she cried, handling the silky robes as if they were contaminated.

'In case you haven't noticed I'm actually black. Y'all ain't never gonna see nothin' but my teeth up there on that stage.'

How I loved her for that; we all agreed, but only Dolette had the balls to say it. The upcoming show in Atlanta was to be filmed for release on video, a perfect opportunity to ditch the black shrouds forever and buy something a little more alluring.

I was learning that to truly succeed as a background vocalist you first needed to understand why you'd been hired. You were there primarily to make the artist look and sound good, and to excel you had to be entirely comfortable with the supportive nature of your role. I'd often witnessed the discomfort of singers at being in the background. Some had taken on the job of backing singer as a stepping stone to becoming an artist in their own right. In general, those that were the greatest successes possessed the ability to work as part of a team and had no desire for their voices or egos to dominate. You had to learn to be humble even if sometimes the main artist was weak.

While shopping in Atlanta, Michelle, Dolette and I stumbled upon a thrift store which stocked a large selection of marching band uniforms. Selecting pieces of uniform we paired them with

Tessa, Michelle Cobbs and Dolette McDonald
backstage on The Police Tour, 1983.

leotards, boots and fishnets, immediately upping the sex factor, though frankly a bin liner would have been more provocative than a burka. Lol Creme and Kevin Godley, former members of the band 10cc and now highly successful film makers, flew out to direct the video. At the stadium shows in Atlanta, Sting, Andy and Stewart thrashed out hit after hit: *Can't Stand Losing You, Message in a Bottle* and the number one hit across the world, *Every Breath You Take.* All three band members were at the zenith of their careers, but cracks in their relationships were beginning to show. Offstage, the boys began to argue and even made the decision to travel in separate limos. Rumours spread quickly that this was likely to be The Police's last tour. Tensions were also growing in my own camp.

'Richard, can you hear me? Hi, how are you? Sorry I haven't called in a while, it's just been so crazy.'

'What, they don't have phones in Texas?'

'Yeah, very funny. It's so hard with the time difference and everything. How's things at home?'

'It's all OK, same old stuff. I've been working on a couple of orchestral arrangements for Trevor Horn so, yeah, but I miss you.'

'I miss you too, this is really hard being away from each other.'

'It is.'

'Erm... the shows are going well, the audiences everywhere are insane and everyone...'

'I called the hotel last night... the phone just rang.'

'Yeah, there's always a party going on... we got back late. Listen, they're calling me to the bus, I've gotta go... I'll call you soon, OK?'

'Yep, speak to you soon.'

'OK, bye.'

I don't think for a minute that I was succeeding in underplaying the fact that I was having a fabulous time on the road. Richard and I were living in different worlds: mine the hedonistic, often surreal world of rock 'n' roll, and his the regular one filled with chores and responsibilities. I was perceived as the partner having all the fun and I suppose this was true, but I was also in America doing a job of work. It was difficult to share stories from the tour as Richard felt excluded. As time went on and the distance between us grew, it became more and more difficult for us to speak to each other.

Whenever wives and partners joined the tour the dynamic within the entourage changed. The entourage lived and worked so closely together that the dynamic became extremely comfortable. When others jumped into 'the family' for a time it changed the atmosphere and felt uncomfortable, particularly for the artists, who relished the freedom they had on the road. It was not that they didn't adore their families, but a touring company becomes a tight-knit unit and the artists felt obligated to behave differently when family were around. Temptations on the road were many and varied, so one tended to adhere to the code 'What happens in Vegas, stays in Vegas'.

The Police tour rolled on throughout the United States, playing to sell-out crowds. In New York the band played at the legendary Shea Stadium, in Los Angeles at the LA Racetrack. During the Shea Stadium sound check Sting and Stewart engaged in a little horseplay: Stewart wrestled Sting over a sound monitor, and Sting cracked a few ribs. By now the press had picked up the rumours that all was not well between Sting, Stewart and Andy, and of course saw this prank as verification.

Tessa, Sting and Dolette backstage at Wembley Arena,
The Police Tour, 1983.

My voice was taking strain from the relentless requirement to sing with no vibrato. Between shows I'd try to rest but my voice was tired and sounded permanently hoarse, and I worried that I might be doing serious damage. When the Synchronicity tour returned to England we played at Wembley Arena with plans to continue the tour into the following year, but for me concerns were rising that having been away from Richard for so long, our relationship was hurting. Not for the first time in my life I faced making a difficult decision, and after much deliberation decided to leave The Police tour after the final shows at Wembley. My first-ever tour had been with the biggest band in the world. Exposed to all the excesses of the world of rock 'n' roll I had survived relatively unscathed, but my relationship and my voice were in trouble and I needed to find out if the damage to both was reversible.

CHAPTER THREE

Behind the stars

Not long after my return to London Richard and I bought a two-bedroomed apartment in Maida Vale. I also consulted a throat specialist who prescribed rest, rest and more rest – even whispering was forbidden. A singer's greatest fear is of developing nodules that grow on the vocal chords and need to be surgically removed. Thankfully no serious damage had been done on tour and in time my voice made a full and complete recovery.

After weeks out of the country, resuming life at home felt strange. On tour, what happened daily was dictated by travel arrangements, sound checks and gigs. The rest of the time was your own, with everything laid on. Someone told you when to wake up and what time to meet for rehearsals or performances. Woe betide you if you had a problem with punctuality, though; it was the job of the tour manager to keep everything running smoothly, and tardiness was not accepted from anyone.

Released from the touring bubble, it took some time to decompress. It was a case of back to reality with a bump: public transport instead of limousines; cooking and cleaning instead of room service and hotels. I missed the glamour and excitement of life on the road. I'd loved touring and hoped that I would have the opportunity to do it again, but was beginning to understand the perils of separation from one's partner for long periods. Being apart had not been easy for Richard or me and it took time for us to feel comfortable in one another's company again. Although understanding, not having been with us in America Richard was unable to relate to many of my experiences and we struggled to feel at ease with each other.

In the interim my reputation as a versatile and reliable singer had grown. I knew of a songwriter named Terry Britten and somehow he had heard of me. I received a call to work on a session for Terry at Mayfair Studios, where he was producing tracks for an album for Tina Turner. An icon from the 60s, Tina was enjoying a revival in popularity thanks to a recent reworking of the song *Let's Stay Together.* Terry played me his track minus Tina's lead vocals. It sounded incredibly strong, with its sexy mid-tempo groove; the song was perfectly constructed and the chorus instantly catchy. Terry and I then routined the backing vocals, which were designed to reinforce Tina's melody. When John Hudson, the recording engineer, added Tina's vocals to the mix it didn't take a genius to realise that this track, *What's Love Got To Do With It?* was something special. It became a smash hit and was never off the radio and television. The album *Private Dancer* re-established Tina Turner as the greatest female rock star in the world, and I became the first choice for many big name record producers. Being credited on Tina's album was the best possible advertising for me and I began to work on a multitude of projects for different producers.

Moving across different styles and genres, often working on three jobs a day, I became a regular choice with producers of radio and TV commercials. With studio time costing in the region of £175 an hour, they hired me for the speed at which I could carry out a brief and execute the vocals they wanted. Quite often I provided the voiceover or tag line at the end of a commercial as well. I found the variety encountered in advertising work stimulating and challenging, as the singer is required to interpret the advertising agency's vision for their product. For Kinder Eggs I became the voice of a green turtle; for Mattel I was a Barbie doll and then the voice of a Cabbage Patch Kid. It was like being an actress, but I mostly used my singing voice. The money was rolling in too. For each commercial I received a fee plus royalties: payments made to the voice artist every time a commercial is aired on radio or viewed on television. Some campaigns ran for months, even years, which meant serious repeat fees.

Richard's parents owned a holiday villa in the south of Spain. He and I decided to spend time there so we could reconnect after the weeks we had been parted. Richard was keen for me to begin recording my own album and was looking around for a record deal. During our holiday I received a phone call.

'Hi is this Tessa?' said a voice.

'Yes it is, who's speaking please?'

'I'm calling to see if you'd like to be involved in the biggest concert that's ever been put on.'

I hated the way the person at the end of the phone hadn't introduced themselves and was unnecessarily cryptic about the event.

It reminded me of the original phone call to meet The Police. I tried not to sound irritated.

'Well, can you tell me a little more about it?'

'I can't tell you who the artist is yet but it's gonna be at Wembley Stadium in July and it's gonna be global. Can't give you details as we don't want it leaking to the press,' rattled off the caller.

'OK... but I'm not in the habit of going to the press, I'm a musician.'

'Listen, I'm sorry, but if you're interested I'll call you in a few days, OK?'

A few days later the mystery concert was revealed in all its glory. The show was to be called Live Aid, a charitable event organised by Bob Geldof and Harvey Goldsmith. I'd be working with David Bowie. I naturally jumped at the opportunity to work with the iconic Mr Bowie, the godfather of glam rock, having long been a fan of his innovative eclectic style influenced by film, art, fashion and literature.

On my return to London I met up with the Bowie band, directed by keyboard player Thomas Dolby. David was involved in every aspect of the Live Aid show and the rehearsals came together swiftly and easily.

'What are you ladies going to wear?' asked the slender Mr Bowie during a break in rehearsals.

'What are you wearing? We'll complement whatever outfit you have,' I said, clearly pleased at being asked.

'I'm gonna wear a pale blue suit so maybe you ladies could find something to go with it? I want you to feel fantastic on that stage,' he said smiling.

David Bowie didn't just look at you with those vastly compelling eyes, he peered into your very soul. This was going to be fun.

'I'm working on the set list,' he said as he sipped on his tea, running a hand through coiffed hair. 'Have you got any ideas for songs?'

'Ooooh yes, yes!' I enthused, bouncing like a human Labrador.' My absolute favourite song is *Rebel Rebel*. Can we do it?'

'Sure, good idea. That'll get the crowd going.'

The set list eventually featured *TVC 15, Rebel Rebel* and *Modern Love*, and closed with *Heroes*. Rehearsal time was tight but within days the band's sound was slick and assured. My wardrobe choice comprised leggings and a diaphanous blue chiffon shirt secured at the collar with a diamanté brooch, a flesh-coloured satin bra, black stilettos and one sheer black glove. I loved the way David was so involved in the visual details of the show as many musicians left the (in their view) less important decisions like clothing to others. During the run-up to Live Aid, David and Mick Jagger recorded a version of *Dancing in the Streets*, and singer Helena Springs and I recorded vocals on the track at Westside Studios. The single became a worldwide hit and featured a video with Jagger and Bowie royally camping things up.

On the morning of 13 July 1985 David and the band left for Wembley Stadium by helicopter. It was a stunning day and Live Aid was being hailed as the biggest gig ever attempted. The concert was organised to raise support for those suffering from the famine in war-torn Ethiopia. A new concept in intercontinental fundraising, almost every major artist and band in the United

States was also taking part, the hope being that the financial and practical input generated jointly by First World communities would make a real difference to thousands who were forgotten, starving and suffering from disease in Africa.

At Wembley Stadium the Bowie band settled in backstage with the other artists. None of us had ever encountered such an array of accomplished musicians at one venue before. Despite it being a charitable event, there was no shortage of performance-enhancing drugs and alcohol on offer. The atmosphere was electric, coupled with the fact that everyone involved believed in the common cause. On TV, Bob Geldof, who had visited Ethiopia and the Sudan, spoke soberly and passionately about what he had witnessed there and implored viewers worldwide to contribute funds to ease the terrible conditions.

Tessa, David Bowie and Helena Springs at Live Aid, Wembley Stadium, 13 July 1985 (Photograph ©PA).

Tessa and David Bowie at Live Aid, Wembley Stadium, 13 July 1985 (Photograph SIPA Press/REX).

We prepared for our set to the sounds of Freddie Mercury and Queen whipping the crowd into a storm. *Radio Gaga* was anthemic, and the crowd responded to Freddie's every cue. I could never have anticipated the feeling of walking out on to the stage that day. David Bowie was masterful, the consummate performer, and from the opening bars he had the 72,000-strong crowd with him. Onstage the sound was fantastic, the band sounded incredible and the collective energy pulsed through each one of us. We pounded through the set finishing off with *Heroes*, a perfect choice lyrically and emotionally. At the close of the concert the artists gathered onstage to sing *Hey Jude*. McCartney, Jagger, Bowie, Sting, Bono, Geldof and the entire cast: an extraordinary line-up for the exhausted but satisfied audience. Live Aid was viewed that day by a global television audience of 1.9 billion people, a third of humanity; a concert that became legendary as 'the day musicians united to raise millions for the underprivileged'.

Needing a home with work space, Richard and I purchased a house in the London suburb of Chiswick. A Victorian semi, it had a small building in the garden which we converted to a studio. Richard's career was flourishing and he was in great demand as an arranger, but what he truly wanted was a break that would lead to success as a producer. He negotiated a recording contract for me to make an album with Rainbow Records, run by the executive Bill Kimber, and began recording tracks for the album. Just about everyone I knew seemed excited about the project, but I harboured feelings that this was not right for me. Richard was responsible for everything to do with the album and made all the musical decisions. With hindsight, I see now that I left too much of my career in my husband's hands and that with a growing reputation of my own as a session singer, the appeal of Richard's vision for me as a recording artist was waning. Where I had once been happy to slot into whatever musical role he had in mind, I was developing an independent persona and beginning to feel stifled by his master plan.

In those days the female session singing industry was small. A select group of vocalists did most of the work and it was hard for young singers to break into it. The rewards were great and no one wanted to let in new blood. If asked to recommend other singers I had no problem suggesting the best person for the job, regardless of whether I felt they might try to steal work from me. I worked on the premise that after working with a producer just once, if someone was able to poach my gigs I hadn't been much good to begin with.

My pal Trevor Horn, producer extraordinaire, had become hugely successful after his work with Frankie Goes to Hollywood put him firmly on the A-list of producers. Who can forget *Relax* and *Two Tribes*? Trevor and his business partner and wife, Jill Sinclair, bought Island Studios in Ladbroke Grove and changed the name to Sarm West. Alongside the recording studio were their record label and publishing company. Trevor, who was producing Grace Jones at the time, asked me to work on *Slave to the Rhythm*, a pop anthem he'd written. Richard was invited to write the orchestral arrangement and given carte blanche on the track; his score was lush and slightly wacky. With a full orchestra behind Grace's unmistakable voice, the vocals and Trevor's production, *Slave to the Rhythm* became a classic of the 80s.

At the time I worked a great deal with Gary Numan of *Are Friends Electric?* and *Cars* fame. Working with Gary was highly creative as he'd often give me a free hand in arranging the vocals. He liked a thick wall of voices on the choruses and would then have me wail or improvise over the end of the track – known as scatting. I enjoyed working with this directive as much as I enjoyed working in a structured format. Some producers were absolutely clear about what they wanted and there was not much room for creativity; others encouraged creative input and allowed me to lead the way. Working with one or more singers was equally creative: the sound of several voices blending hugely satisfying and the sound of a full choir truly spectacular. The Steven Spielberg movie *An American Tail*, which involved animated mice, required a full orchestra and choir. The voices were recorded at Abbey Road Studios and I can honestly say that you would not have heard better sounding mice anywhere!

Gary Numan collaborated on an album with the keyboard player from Shakatak, Bill Sharp. The album spawned a hit for the two of them called *Change Your Mind*. I sang on the track and performed with them on *Top of the Pops*. Bill then asked me to sing the lead vocal on a track of his called *Famous People*, and he and I made a video to promote it. I had yet to learn how to take full control of my career and remember the make-up artist on the shoot insisting that I wear a combination of blue, yellow and green eye make-up. She must have applied it with a garden trowel because instead of looking sexy and glamorous I looked as if I'd gone ten rounds with Mike Tyson. I knew full well that the make-up was horrible, but instead of explaining that it was not the look I'd had in mind, and too inhibited to say no, I said nothing – a pattern of behaviour that would not serve me well.

Bill Sharpe and Tessa promo pic for Famous People single, 1985.

Now fully into producing my solo album, Richard's recording involved some of London's finest musicians and singers. Control of the results being entirely in his hands, deep down I was unhappy with the musical journey I was on, but at no time during the recording did I voice my doubts; I chose instead to go along with what I knew felt wrong. It was a behaviour pattern that would repeat itself on many occasions. Everyone seemed to have such faith in me that I feared letting Richard down and others who believed in me. But where was my faith in myself? I was fast becoming a success but struggling to find my own voice. I enjoyed singing the lead vocal on tracks but it was becoming clear to me that my real strengths lay in providing support for others. My ego was healthy enough, but I wasn't sure I had the relentless ambition and drive a solo artiste needs to remain in the spotlight. I loved performing, but was coming to the conclusion that you could shine in the background as well as centre stage. While people around me were busy investing in my future, I needed to face up to what I wanted for myself.

My first solo single, *The President's Girl*, launched in the UK in 1985; in the accompanying poster campaign, wrapped only in the star spangled banner, I proclaimed an affair with an American president years before the infamous 'Monicagate' scandal. After seeing one of the posters around town I was contacted by David Mindel, the owner of Mingles Music, one of London's most successful jingle companies. David and I went on to work together on radio and TV commericals for many years to come. I was surprised at how good it felt to be promoting my own product, but in spite of extensive promoting the single failed to make it into the charts. Still not fully in the driver's seat of my career, I continued to allow crucial decisions to be made by others. Again and again the issue of who should have been in charge of my career came up, and remained unresolved. I responded by burying my concerns deeper.

Tessa posing for The President's Girl single, released in 1985.

CHAPTER FOUR

The glitter trail

In line with the concept that 'she who leaves a trail of glitter will never be forgotten' I experimented with as many 80s fashion looks as possible, from oversized mohair sweaters that revealed one bare shoulder to batwing sleeved Lycra dresses paired with leggings and high heels. Scrunched into stiff curls, my heavily moussed hair cascaded on to oversized shoulder pads, and every outfit was topped off with huge earrings. One of my favourite outfits was a cropped leather jacket worn with biker shorts and knee socks. Well, it was the 80s...

Early 1986 saw my return to Mayfair Studios to record vocals on Tina Turner's new album. The A side was produced entirely by Graham Lyle and Terry Britten, the team behind *What's Love Got To Do With It?* The songs were fantastic, but the standout track for me was the punchy *Typical Male*, with Phil Collins on drums and Tina's edgy vocals. I then added my parts to an already killer track. The album reached number two in the UK chart and number four on the Billboard chart that same year. To hear

Tessa, 1986 (Photograph: Mike Prior).

myself performing alongside great artists and musicians was a dream come true, although having worked on two hit albums for Tina, I had yet to meet her as my vocals were recorded at the end of the album process, after Tina had already recorded hers. Each aspect of an album process being added over a period of time, the participating musicians seldom met each other.

Some months later I was introduced to the singer Katie Kissoon at a vocal session for disco legend Gloria Gaynor. I loved the sound of Katie's sweet and soulful voice and was struck by the gentleness of her personality. From the beginning, singing along-side Katie was easy; she had no desire to dominate or take control, and listened carefully to the producer's directive. She was beautiful. Her dark hair fell in ringlets and she walked effortlessly in skyscraper heels. The two of us worked out the vocal parts so comfortably and easily that day it was as if we had always known one another. Not long after, Katie invited me to work with her on a project for the guitar legend Eric Clapton. Eric was recording his tenth studio album, *August*, with Phil Collins. The producer, a long-time Clapton associate, was Tom O'Dowd.

Katie and I had a chance to get to know each other better as we drove down from London to the residential studio.

'We went to school together, Phil and I,' Katie said as we sped through the leafy Surrey countryside. 'I met Eric when we both worked on the Roger Waters tour. He wasn't in the best space on that gig but we've always stayed in touch.'

'I know Eric has battled a fair few demons but I understand he's doing well now,' I said.

'Yes, he's doing really well and thinks he might go out on the road after this recording.'

'Funny how you and I met on the Gloria Gaynor session such a short time ago and here we are winging our way to sing with your mates,' I laughed. 'Thank you for thinking of me, Katie, I'm well aware that you could have chosen anyone to work with so I'm really grateful.'

'You're welcome, sometimes you just get a feeling about people.'

The car swung left through an imposing set of gates and continued down a rhododendron-lined driveway.

Eric and Phil were waiting outside the studio greeting us as we arrived.

'Ladies, so good of you to come,' Phil joked as he gave us both a bear hug. 'Sorry about this little shack we're recording in, bit of a dive I know.'

Eric, who looked tanned and fit, said, 'How are you, ladies? Thank you for coming all this way. Nice to meet you, Tessa.'

The studio was state-of-the-art gorgeous. Cups of tea were organised and Eric, Phil, producer Tom Dowd, Katie and I began work on the business of the day. After listening to the tracks the vocal arrangements came together quickly. *Holy Mother*, a heart-wrenching ballad had Eric in his inimitable style, crying out for redemption.

'I need you to sound celestial on this,' he said, drawing heavily on his cigarette. Strumming the chords for the bridge section, Eric sang an idea for the vocal part.

'If I sing the first line can you somehow repeat what I'm singing?'

Katie and I swiftly picked up what was needed and without discussion sang the harmony parts. Amazing that when musicians are in sync with each other very few words are needed.

On the upbeat *Behind the Mask* Katie and I sang the choruses with Phil. For me, this was pure vocal heaven and didn't feel like work. Eric and Phil were in high spirits as the day's background vocals added sparkle to their album, which was now virtually complete. At the time I did not realise that working on *August* heralded the start of a long association with Katie Kissoon and the blues rocker Eric Clapton.

Growing up, I felt I'd missed out on the golden age of disco. Too young to strut my funky stuff in a nightclub, it didn't stop me from loving the music of Donna Summer, Earth Wind and Fire and the ultimate good time band, Chic. Chic's vocals were always stunning and I discovered that the girls in the band were chosen from the cream of the New York session scene, so when I got a call to work with Chic founder member Nile Rogers, I was ecstatic. We met at Air Studios in London to work on tracks for the pop princes, Duran Duran. Nile was uber-cool and knew exactly what he wanted to hear from me on the disco-inspired track *Notorious*. Uncharacteristically funky, this was something of a departure for the Duran Duran boys, with its heavy bass riff, popping brass and Nile Rogers' signature rhythm guitar. Yes indeed, Duran Duran had been anointed with the funk from the undisputed king of disco! Nile wanted a vocal sound effect over the intro of the song, and after running a few different things I tried a sharp intake of breath. So simple, but so effective, and exactly what Nile was after. I then doubled up the chorus vocals with lead singer Simon Le Bon and Nile was happy, but I couldn't help feeling I hadn't done enough to impress him. My fears were unfounded though; *Notorious* became a massive hit in the US, reaching number two on the Billboard chart.

I first met the singer/songwriter Richard Darbyshire in his home town of Manchester. After hearing his rich, soulful vocals on beautifully crafted songs, I tried to work with him whenever possible on his own projects and on backing vocal sessions. Richard and his band, Living in a Box, released their eponymous debut single, *Living in a Box*, in 1987 and it reached number five in the UK. I toured extensively with the band, singing and miming the bass guitar on television shows across Europe.

At the same time my husband, Richard, began collaborating with Paul McCartney on reworking some old Wings tracks. While they were at it, Paul asked Richard to help out with an idea for his wife Linda's 45th birthday; he wanted to record a song and press

Living in a Box, (L to R) Richard Darbyshire, Anthony Critchlow, Josephine Campbell, Tessa Niles and (centre) Marcus Vere, 1988.

a 45 rpm disc for her as a gift. In the 1950s, Linda McCartney's father had been a successful music publisher. Legend has it that after visiting the Eastman family home, the songwriter Jack Lawrence wrote and dedicated a song to Linda, titled *Linda*, as a thank you to her father. Paul had managed to track down the song and asked Richard to write arrangements for two different versions: for the A side, a big band swing rendition, and a thundering Latin one for the B side with Paul, of course, on lead vocals. Working over one hectic weekend, Richard did a superb job on both arrangements and the tracks were recorded and mixed.

Paul McCartney, Richard Darbyshire and I had a ball, singing together. Totally unpretentious, Paul picked up a nearby guitar during a break in recording and began strumming a familiar Beatles song.

'That boy, took my love away,' sang Paul softly.

'Though he'll regret it someday.'

'But this boy wants you back again.'

Desperate to appear nonchalant, the truth was that Richard Darbyshire and I couldn't wait to jump in with the harmonies on this iconic song from our childhood. For Richard, the experience could not be overestimated; it was a moment akin to an aspiring painter sitting next to Picasso and watching him sketch.

'This boy, wouldn't mind the pain.'

'Would always feel the same.'

'If this boy gets you back again.'

'Well now, that's a blast from the past,' McCartney chuckled as he let the final chord ring.

'Yep they don't write them like that anymore,' I said, grinning at Richard.

It was hard not to be overwhelmed by the mind-blowing situation, Paul McCartney casually playing the songs that had inspired thousands of kids to become musicians. I had the feeling that Paul knew exactly the effect he was having on Richard D, but it was only after the sessions had finished that my dear friend completely lost his composure. Standing in a quiet corridor outside the studio he grabbed me by the shoulders, his eyes popping with exultation.

'Tessa Niles! I don't think you quite understand what just happened in there, we've just been singing with a fucking Beatle!'

Katie Kissoon and I met up again with Eric Clapton when his single *Behind the Mask* was released from the *August* album. For the *Top of the Pops* television performance, Katie and I wore tight black Lycra dresses, the fashion weapon of choice for most background singers during the 1980s. The small temporary stage at the BBC was constructed of blocks, and during the recording

Katie somehow managed to get the heel of one shoe wedged in a gap between them. With the cameras rolling, unable to extricate her shoe, Katie had to pivot as best she could on her trapped heel. A short time later Eric invited Katie and me to join his all-star touring band, which included some of the finest musicians ever to grace a stage: Steve Ferrone on drums, Nathan East on bass and Greg Phillanganes on keyboards – the big three of America's session musicians. Steve had moved to the States from Britain after achieving success with The Average White Band, and gone on to become the drummer of choice for many artists. Nathan had worked on thousands of projects ranging from Michael Jackson to Phil Collins and could handle genres from blues to jazz and from pop to rock. Greg had played in Stevie Wonder's band and was highly respected in the session world. Together, they had taken session playing to a new level, and like the 80s supermodels, had become recognised personalities in their own right. Highly skilled, confident and at ease, they were at the very top of their game. The percussionist Ray Cooper completed Eric's touring ensemble. A charismatic performer whose energetic and intense solos wowed audiences worldwide, he had worked with The Rolling Stones and toured with Elton John. Katie and I were keeping illustrious company with these musicians. The Eric Clapton Band European Tour began in Manchester and ended in Florence. An amazing synergy of personalities and musicianship, it was a team that went on to make musical history for years. Our boss thought so too.

Between touring with Eric, my friends Dolette McDonald (from The Police/Synchronicity tour of the US), Johannesburg-born Miriam Stockley and I began work with ABC on tracks for their new album, *Alphabet City*. The band had taken time off while lead singer Martin Fry was successfully treated for Hodgkin's disease, but was back with a vengeance. The album was produced by band members Mark White and Martin Fry in conjunction with Bernard Edwards, best known for his work with my favourite band, Chic. Singing with Dolette and Miriam was an absolute treat as we worked our own magic on the nostalgic track *When Smokey Sings*, a tribute to the soul singer Smokey Robinson that reached number five in the US chart. In the video and subsequent TV performances of the song, however, ABC hired models to mime to our voices. Until this point the Musicians Union had been able to protect members against this kind of thing: miming was disallowed without the written permission of the original performers. Dolette, Miriam and I had certainly not given permission for our vocals to be mimed to, but the union's voice no longer carried weight with the record companies, who wanted the freedom to use anyone they liked. Despite vehement protest from its members, the union could do nothing to protect us, an incident that signalled a change in the way session musicians were treated. Bands signed to record labels also wanted to be able to use anyone they liked to help promote their product, and for bona fide musicians to have non-musicians miming to our performances was a slap in the face.

During a visit to Berlin in 1987, the US President, Ronald Reagan, challenged Soviet premier Mikhail Gorbachev to tear down the Berlin Wall. In the music world Whitney Houston sang *I Wanna Dance with Somebody,* and Rick Astley was making perfect pop with *Never Gonna Give You Up*. Richard Niles, who had always dreamed of forming a jazz big band to perform his own compositions, named his new baby Bandzilla. Richard's tunes and complex signature arrangements stretched the players' capabilities to the max. His band included the finest young session musicians in London and though the tunes were largely instrumental, singer Clive Griffin and I provided vocals on some tracks. Bandzilla featured as the house band on comedienne Ruby Wax's television series *Don't Miss Wax*. Richard's arranging skills were also used by Trevor Horn for an album by the pop duo The Pet Shop Boys; a dance album featuring their signature electronics, Trevor added live musicians to transform their sound from synth pop to orchestral. I sang vocals on *It's Alright*, a tale of political and environmental issues wrapped up in a shiny three-and-a-half-minute pop format – The Pet Shop Boys always pushed boundaries with their music.

From way back I'd been a fan of Steve Winwood's music. Steve's brand of blue-eyed soul was enjoying renewed popularity after the success of his previous album that featured the hit single *Higher Love,* so it was great to be asked to work on tracks for his next album, *Roll with It.* Virtuoso session singer Mark Williamson and I spent the day in Steve's residential studio. Working with Mark was great and the vocals came together effortlessly. Softly spoken Steve, still with the tiniest trace of Brummie accent, was clear about what he wanted from us, and after a long day's work was very happy with the results. Backing vocals add colour and dynamics to songs; imagine how Aretha Franklin's *Respect* would have sounded without the anthemic, 'Just a little bit, just a little bit' background vocals, or the Beach Boys' 'Bar Bar Bar, Bar Barbara Ann'. The use of harmonies in a song enables certain sections to shine, often driving home the chorus part, or 'hook'. *Roll with It* reached number one in the US chart and the single *Don't You Know What the Night Can Do?* was used for a Michelob beer campaign on US television. Later that year I received a substantial royalty payment for the use of the commercial. Not only was my career in music fulfilling my dreams, it was keeping my bank manager happy.

Richard and I continued working at a furious pace, to the point where we'd often pass each other on the stairs of our home, me returning from a job and he leaving for one. I was now 27 years old and Richard 37. We had no plans to start a family and were both relentlessly driving our careers forward. Ambition occupied our entire focus, and for me the need for Richard's mentorship was becoming less and less. I was forging my own path through the session world. Undoubtedly Richard had opened many doors for me in the beginning and had provided an abundance of opportunities, but I no longer wanted or needed that kind of help. I had deep concerns about the musical path I was pursuing with my personal career, but no idea how to raise them. Rainbow Records had folded before my solo album could be released, but work as a session singer was keeping me busy night and day. On a typical day I recorded TV jingles and worked on album sessions, sometimes covering as many as four sessions a day. One session constituted a minimum of three hours' work, and a jingle would normally take between one and two hours to complete. I'd then dash across London to the next job.

In between the studio dates I toured with Eric Clapton. As tour bands do, the members bonded closely musically and on a personal level. Katie and I had become extremely good friends by this time and road life had its own ebb and flow, although we left the partying to experts like the mischievous Steve Ferrone and keyboard player Alan Clark who formed a charming but boisterous alliance. On the road there was always a party going on somewhere; a record company or promoter hosting a lavish bash after the show or a musician simply cracking open the mini bar in their room was excuse enough. Something kicked off in every city; people wanted to party with the band and the band loved to party with people. Women and drugs were plentiful and readily available, and it was accepted that the guys would party hard. Finding himself languishing in a jail cell after one such night of debauchery, Steve Ferrone left a mournful message on Eric's manager's answer phone: channelling his inner Paul Robeson, Steve sang 'Nobody knows the trouble I seen, nobody knows my sorrow...' We dined out on Steve's story for quite a while.

January 1988 brought with it the Eric Clapton 25th Anniversary Tour, and we were joined by Elton John and Mark Knopfler. The tour began in the UK, continued throughout Europe and the United States for most of the year and finished in Japan. The addition of Elton and Mark to the band was welcomed and their songs interspersed with Eric's set. *Money for Nothing, Solid Rock, I'm Still Standing* and *Saturday Night's Alright for Fighting* never failed to please and Eric's searing guitar solos on *Cocaine* and *Layla* delighted audiences night after night. In the thundering duet *Tearing Us Apart*, Eric and Katie sang together while Nathan, Greg and I threw our finest moves at the ecstatic crowds. The gigs were amazing and Eric was on top form. Public opinion always placed his vocals second to his guitar playing, but the truth is he's also a fantastic singer and I loved to tell him this after the shows. Eric was genuinely surprised to be praised for his voice.

The Eric Clapton band plus a star-studded cast that included Peter Gabriel, The Bee Gees, Phil Collins and Leonard Cohen were booked to perform at The Royal Albert Hall for The Prince's Trust Rock Gala. Prince Charles is patron of the charity that helps change young lives by giving practical and financial support. Eric was joined on stage by Elton John and Mark Knopfler. Before the show, Eric stood in a line-up backstage to meet Prince Charles and Princess Diana. Eric later told the band that he'd engaged in a conversation with the Prince about tailors.

'Your Royal Highness, I'm interested to know where you go to get your suits made.'

To which Prince Charles responded, 'Well to be honest, Eric, I don't really go to them... they come to me.'

The Gala was magnificent. Joe Cocker blew the audience away with his version of *With a Little Help from My Friends*, although the lead singer of pop outfit Wet Wet Wet embarrassed himself by trying to out-sing Joe during the song. So wrong! In the box

The Eric Clapton band with Prince Charles and Princess Diana,
The Prince's Trust Gala, Royal Albert Hall, 1988.

opposite the stage was the royal couple. Dressed in a yellow satin suit, Diana sat sedately with her handbag on her lap. The princess retained complete composure until Phil Collins came on stage to perform, at which point she could no longer hold herself back; quickly passing her handbag to her lady-in-waiting she leapt up from her seat and began to dance like a teenager to *You Can't Hurry Love*. The Albert Hall was electrified and the audience erupted. From the stage I could see that Charles, conditioned from childhood, remained firmly in his seat, but his young wife wowed the crowd. It's impossible to exaggerate how spectacularly different it was back then for a member of the royal family to break with tradition and let themselves go. From the look of things that night, 'we' were not amused.

During a break from the Clapton tour in June that year I was asked to put together a crack vocal team to perform at the Nelson Mandela 70th Birthday Tribute, to be held at Wembley Stadium. I chose Lance Ellington, Katie Kissoon, Jonn Savannah, Carole Kenyon and Katie's brother, Mac Kissoon. The event was designed to raise worldwide awareness of the imprisonment of Nelson Mandela and a bid to try to force the then Nationalist South African government to grant Mandela and other political prisoners held on Robben Island an early release. The concert became the pop-political event of all time. The night before, I went to visit my friend Dolette who was touring with Sting's band. When I arrived at the hotel, Sting insisted that I join him and the band in opening the show. I was thrilled and quickly ran home to learn *Set Them Free, They Dance Alone, Message in a Bottle* and rehearse *Every Breath You Take*, which I hadn't sung since the Synchronicity tour. The vocal team I'd put together would be backing 'the soul set', performing later in the day. This team comprised Natalie Cole, Joe Cocker, The Rev Al Green, Jonathan Butler (a Capetonian), Ashford and Simpson, and Freddie Jackson. My team of singers didn't have much time to learn and rehearse the artists' songs before the event, but thankfully everyone did their homework and was up to speed on the day.

At the start of the Birthday Tribute, the veteran actor and human rights activist Harry Belafonte introduced Sting to a packed Wembley Stadium and the band opened with a rousing version of the appropriately titled *Set Them Free*. Sting's second song was an emotional version of the ballad *They Dance Alone*. As I looked out over the vast crowds, singing the words 'One day we'll sing our freedom', a light wind blew across the stage and my eyes began to stream with tears. The song tells the tale of Chilean women mourning their missing loved ones and dancing the cueca while holding photos of 'the disappeared'. It was impossible not to be touched by both the music and the message, and the power of the collective has never failed to move me. Sting's set was a resounding success. George Michael and the Eurythmics then performed their sets, and after an introduction by comedian Lenny Henry, Al Green kicked off the soul set with a heartfelt version of his classic hit *Let's Stay Together*. When Natalie Cole began to sing *He's Got the Whole World in His Hands*, a bright window in an otherwise overcast sky opened, and the sun shone on the stadium. The crowd erupted. The estimated TV audience for the concert was over 600 million in 67 countries, and news of its popularity reached Mandela and his fellow political prisoners. The apartheid government did not allow the event to be broadcast in South Africa.

Tessa, 1988.

The Eric Clapton Tour featuring Mark Knopfler and Elton John resumed in September, beginning in Dallas, Texas, travelling across the country and into Canada, finishing in Calgary, Alberta. In November the band flew to Japan to perform five shows.

The Japanese economy was booming in the late 80s and the neon-clad shops in Tokyo overflowed with the latest gadgets and goods. Getting around the city was easy in the immaculately kept taxis, where the drivers wore crisp white gloves and offered customers the use of the latest fax machine or photocopier. From the crowded noodle bars plastered with film posters in Shinjuku to the parks with their formal gardens and street performers, the city buzzed from morning till night. Buddhist shrines nestled next to restaurants that displayed realistic plastic replicas of their dishes under fluorescent lights. On every street corner vending machines pumped out cans of sickly sweet coffee, and on giant billboards pre-pubescent girls advertised everything from make-up to Walkmans. In the department stores exquisitely dressed women bowed low and greeted customers. Western-style shops featured elaborate window displays, one of which was a Japanese take on the Nativity, perfect in every detail other than a jolly Santa Claus on a snow-topped hill, nailed to a cross. I had an incredible time discovering the extraordinary sights and culture of Japan, but it was the relationship with my husband that urgently required my attention.

Again, the time spent away from Richard had taken its toll. I'd been on the road for most of the year and neither Richard nor I knew how to broach the problems that had developed from spending so much time apart. It was as if we had both decided to bury our troubles rather than discuss them, but the deeper we buried them, the more insurmountable the problems seemed. Phone calls home became fewer and increasingly more uncomfortable and although we both tried to carry on as normal, each time I returned from my travels I knew it would be harder and harder to settle back into being a couple. I had more in common with my 'family' on the road than with my husband. Our relationship was in deep trouble but neither of us wanted to admit it.

To some extent the tour dates in Japan were a distraction from the problems at home, but the band knew we were coming to the end of a highly successful period and felt the impending loss of not being together. It had been an incredible year; no one voiced it, but we all knew the tour had taken its toll on us one way or another.

*The Eric Clapton band at Saturday Night Live, 1990,
(L to R) Nathan East, Katie Kissoon, Phil Palmer, Eric Clapton, Greg Phillanganes, Alan Clark,
Tessa Niles and (centre) Steve Ferrone
(Photograph: Edie Baskin).*

Sting and his band were performing in Tokyo at the same time, and on our night off we all went to watch his show. Backstage at the Tokyo Dome I was to hang out with Dolette but before that I went to see my ex-boss.

'Tessa Niles, what are you doing here?' Sting said as he lifted me up and spun me round his large empty dressing room. I flashed back to the embarrassing moment in his house a few years before when I'd misread his humour.

'Oh you know, earning a crust with a bunch of lowlifes. Someone's gotta do it, right?'

'How's Eric doing? I hear he's on the road with my friend Knopfler.'

Even under the unforgiving light in the dressing room Sting was extraordinarily handsome.

'Yes, we're at the end of the tour, it's been amazing. Listen I don't want to keep you, I just wanted to say good luck for the show. Have a good one.'

I blew him a kiss and turned to leave.

'Will you come up and sing on *Every Breath*?' Sting called out

'Absolutely... would love to.'

During the show I sat with Mark Knopfler on a flight case at the side of the stage watching Sting and his musicians spin their magic. I joined them on stage for the final encore of *Every Breath You Take,* and was suddenly overcome by emotions I'd been trying hard for too long to keep in check – emotions I had not dared to admit. I knew then that I had been denying the fact that my relationship with Richard was over. The admission had taken a long time to surface, but I knew it was the truth.

After the show the two bands were taken to a nightclub in the famous Roppongi district of Tokyo. The club was full of international fashion models and the boys were happier than kids in a sweet shop. Perhaps it was the relief of having finally faced my fears, but I felt more powerful than I ever remembered feeling before. Yes, there would be problems to face on my return to London, but this particular night in Tokyo was not going to pass unmarked.

Dolette and I partied as if our lives depended on it. Release from the tension I had been burdened with for months washed over me like an epiphany as I realised that at last I'd found the strength to change my circumstances. Intoxicated with the mix of adrenalin and self-realisation, I was joined on the dance floor by a handsome stranger. The energy between us was tangible – as if an electrical switch had been thrown – and in the early hours of the following morning after leaving a scribbled a note on the bathroom mirror I quietly let myself out of his hotel room.

Plans to host a family Christmas loomed in London, and with only a few days to make the necessary arrangements I felt it would be best to wait until after the holidays to discuss things with Richard. My resolve to postpone matters of the heart lasted for exactly one day after my arrival; I could no longer hold back the emotions I'd been bottling up for so long. 'We need to talk, Richard,' I announced

I could see by the look on his face that this declaration came as no surprise.

'Go ahead,' Richard said as he sat down.

'Look, I know this is bad timing but we really need to discuss some things. It's obvious you're not happy and I'm definitely not happy either.'

With no prior thought as to what I would say, I poured out my feelings into the early hours of the morning. I hadn't intended to end the relationship that night just before Christmas, but years of living with doubt and the inability to express myself culminated in one massive declaration of finality. I must have sounded resolute in my decision to end the relationship as Richard made no real attempt to change my mind or persuade me that we should both try and fight for our marriage. He didn't question me on much at all, and there was no recrimination or any real anger from him.

Without raised voices or accusations, seven years of marriage evaporated. Perhaps Richard was too shocked and hurt to say anything, perhaps he too was relieved. Neither of us suggested a cooling-off period to think things over and reflect on the enormity of our decision, although we chose not to say anything to anyone until Christmas was over. Looking back, my timing sucked; to think that it would be anything but torturous to try to act normally after dropping such a bombshell was naïve, and even heartless. We did it somehow, acting our painful roles until the festivities were over. Richard was a good man who had not deserved a relationship with someone too immature to be married. I would have liked to blame being on the road for the break-up, but although this was a component of our difficulties, it was not the only reason. Our age difference had been more of a problem than we'd cared to admit, for at 38 Richard was ready for more commitment than I felt able to give. What he saw as guidance I viewed as controlling, and what he viewed as loving I found stifling. Now 28, I had grown up inside the marriage but had not matured. Richard had always been a strong supporter of my career, but both of us had been so busy building empires that we had allowed ambition to overshadow our relationship.

In January 1989 Richard Niles and I went our separate ways. I moved out of our Chiswick house and moved in with my good friend Pepi and her two children, Gabrielle and Danielle. I had not the slightest doubt that I had made the right decision; the truth was I had stayed in the marriage for longer than I should, and felt an enormous sense of relief. Financially thriving, I relished the challenge of starting over. It was high time to take control of my life.

CHAPTER FIVE
Out of Africa

'Take it all off and dye it white please.'

The hairdresser was unperturbed by my request. Clearly just another day working in Covent Garden's trendiest salon.

'Certainly,' he said, removing his scissors from their sheath. 'Is madam going Annie Lennox androgynous or the Madonna crop?'

To my mind a new beginning should herald a new look. The new 'I don't need a man in my life' do was just the ticket. Sure, it was reactionary. It was me taking a stand and stating that my life and my choices were now my own.

I loved living at Pepi's house. Moving in with her and her girls was like going home; her love and support were unfailing. Leaving school at 16 meant I'd never experienced communal life, boarding school or university, so the changes I was undergoing came as no surprise to my friend, who had questioned the wisdom of my marriage from the start.

Pepi and Tessa, 1989.

Stephanie Bloomstein was born to Jewish immigrant parents in Hackney, in the East End of London. Her father left when she was young and her struggling mother became fiercely ambitious for her two children. Stephanie's older brother Rex moved towards a career in television and broadcasting, while Pepi learned the art of song and dance. A jazz singer at heart, she had sung a myriad of styles in her time and was now working the functions circuit. She didn't like it, life as a single mother of two was hard and the gigs fed neither her soul nor her kids.

She'd married young and become ensconced in a Bohemian community in north London, raising her two children, making bread and a name for herself in the world of jazz. Petite, full of personality and a meteorite of creative energy, Pepi often used her self-deprecating humour as a shield against the world. Our backgrounds were polar opposites, and she and I often wondered why we'd been drawn to each other. Over time, my beloved friend taught me Yiddish, an appreciation of all things vintage and the meaning of loyalty. I have always been attracted to the innate strength of Jewish women and their resilience to hardship. When it came to keeping family and friends together, Pepi had rock-like strength. She possessed the strongest life force of anyone I had ever encountered; giving love was her *raison d'être*, the glue that kept everyone around her connected.

Living with Pepi for a few months allowed me to consider my future. My bank account was healthy, so I decided to purchase my own house. In the west London suburb of Chiswick I fell for a handsome three-bedroomed Edwardian house with high-ceilinged rooms in leafy, lovely Woodstock Road. It needed renovation, but a new kitchen and updates to the bathrooms would come in time. In spite of moving in with nothing but my clothes and an antique brass bed, my new house became my sanctuary.

Against a backdrop of the Tiananmen Square protests in China and recession fears as British stock market prices continued to fall, my session career flourished. Julian Mendelsohn, producer of The Pet Shop Boys, invited me to sing on tracks they were busy with for the American actress and singer Liza Minnelli. The Pet Shop Boys' front man Neil Tennant's bitingly acerbic observations, and his partner Chris Lowe's unusual slant on electronic music pushed the envelope of mainstream pop, and the *Results* album successfully paired Liza's powerful Broadway-style vocals with a synthesized 80s beat. Their great disco version of the Tanita Tickeram hit *Twist in My Sobriety* reached number six in the UK album chart.

Tears for Fears, another hugely talented male duo at the time, brought Carol Kenyon, Dolette McDonald and me together as a vocal team on tracks for their *Seeds of Love* album. Roland Orzabal and Curt Smith had spent years and reportedly a million pounds recording the tracks, which featured a wide range of influences while retaining the band's instantly identifiable sound. *Sowing the Seeds of Love* was a homage to the group's love of Beatles music, and *Year of the Knife* echoed a stadium rock tune. Dolette and I went down to Peter Gabriel's Real World Studio in Bath to record, and Carol and I worked on tracks in London at Mayfair Studios. The songs featured outstanding musicians: Phil Collins, Pino Paladino, songwriter Nicky Holland and a previously unknown singer and pianist, Oleta Adams. While on tour in America, Roland and Curt had discovered Oleta performing her nightly set in the bar of their Kansas City hotel. Her achingly beautiful voice was rich with soul, influenced by jazz and gospel music. Blown away by Oleta's extraordinary talent, Roland and Kurt promised that they would include her in their next recording venture. How Oleta's voice blended with Roland's full-timbre vocals during the recording of *Seeds of Love* was particularly special. In the studio, Roland, a perfectionist, knew exactly what he wanted to hear and gave inexhaustible attention to detail. On the track *Swords and Knives* I recorded dozens of takes until he was satisfied. The track began with our two voices singing octaves apart with a haunting piano accompaniment; it then built into a lush, complex arrangement and finally returned to just piano and vocals. It is still one of my all-time favourites. The *Seeds of Love* album reached a Top Ten position in many countries and launched the solo career of Oleta Adams.

By 1989 The Rolling Stones had been making music together for 27 years and the making of the *Steel Wheels* album is said to have repaired the relationship of Keith Richards and Mick Jagger. With veteran producer Chris Kimsey at the helm, singer Sonia Jones and I fired off rock vocals on pounding tracks. Mick was his usual ebullient self in the studio while Sonia and I sang.

Backing singers constantly had to adapt to working in different musical genres. Vocal versatility was a given, but each type of music also had a visual look. For a rock 'n' roll session it was important to dress with a frisson of sex, whereas for a jingle or choir session it was not necessary to wear full basque and stilettos. For a live performance one needed to up the style, of course, and in Eric Clapton's band Katie and I were given a free hand in choosing what to wear. For the most part this worked well, as we both knew what looked good on stage. But on one occasion, tired of wearing black, we had brightly coloured chiffon dresses made, floaty numbers that were a distinct departure from our usual LBDs. They were not a success. Katie's dress was just about passable, but in mine I resembled an inverted fuchsia cupcake. Mercifully, few photos have reared their ugly heads, and in the sage words of pint-sized designer Karl Lagerfeld, 'One is never overdressed or underdressed in a little black dress.' The memory of another wardrobe malfunction in Dubai, while performing with The Shades of Love, has never left me. The fabric of my beautiful aquamarine dress by the British designer Anthony Price was draped skilfully around a boned corset, but the temperatures in Dubai remained scorching even at night, and with the additional heat generated by the spotlights on stage, performing was an altogether sweaty experience. During the opening number of the show I raised my arms with gusto but the corset stayed put and, springing up with my arms, my breasts popped out over the top of the corset. Lost in the music, while singing the words 'I just wanna be free' I had not noticed or felt this happen; when I eventually did, 'the puppies' were popped back into place and securely contained, it being the Middle East!

Tessa in the Anthony Price dress, 1989.

Work with Eric Clapton continued in 1989 and the band recorded his 11th studio album, *Journeyman*. Joining Eric, an illustrious cast included George Harrison, Phil Collins and vocals by Chaka Khan, Darryl Hall and Linda Womack. Katie and I provided vocals on the single *Bad Love*, which earned Eric the Best Male Rock Vocal Performance at the Grammy Awards the following year. For me, life was amazing. It felt so good to be single; I was loving living on my own and had no desire to jump into a new relationship. My financial house was in order, helped immeasurably by my secretary, Fiona Sanders-Reece. Initially Fi had worked for Richard and me as a bookkeeper, but over time she became much more and now acted as a manager and friend, taking care of all aspects of my work life from studio bookings to overseeing tax issues and, of course, the all-important invoicing of clients. After recording *Journeyman*, the Eric Clapton band embarked on a tour to promote the album. I had no idea at the time that this tour would be life-altering for me. It began as usual with a series of sold-out shows at The Royal Albert Hall in London. Eric loved the famous domed auditorium and performed there every year. That year he included guest appearances from Mark Knopfler and Carole King, and split the run of shows so that he worked first with a four-piece blues band, later augmented with the touring band.

Getting along with the boss's wife or girlfriend is a given in any business and was imperative in a group that worked closely together. For the most part this was never a problem as the ladies in question were not around for long. Eric's former wife, Pattie Boyd, was delightful; a highly successful model in the 1960s she had bewitched and married Beatle George Harrison before marrying Eric. However, Eric's then girlfriend, an Italian model, Lory Del Santo, seemed reluctant to form any kind of relationship with Katie and me. Perhaps she viewed us as a threat, but it's more likely that she and Eric were already having problems in their relationship. It was difficult to gauge what made Eric happy. Even though I'd spent a lot of time with him he was often introspective and distant, and his well-documented battle with drugs and alcohol continued to plague him. For Eric, many of the uncomfortable or just plain tedious things in everyday life that ordinary mortals have to deal with were taken care of by others. When you've been famous for as many years as he has, you are surrounded by people who are only too willing to assist. You can delegate anything to anyone, from everyday chores like banking and paying bills to the removal of unwanted girlfriends and groupies. You can employ someone to do whatever you do not care to do, so issues requiring a one-on-one emotional response, or having to deal with difficulties, make for tricky moments. This was something that Eric would address later in his life, but at that point his manager, Roger Forrester, took care of any 'unpleasantries', which absolved Eric from many responsibilities. Roger held a powerful position and in many ways I felt sorry for Lory, although she made no attempt to be friendly and had a particularly unpleasant habit of looking you up and down. Not a cursory glance but a long, lingering stare. Katie and I tried hard to get to know Lory but she remained distant. She and Eric had had a child together, a beautiful boy named Conor. I knew Eric had wanted to become a father, but he struggled with the selfless attention-giving that parenting demands, and not having known his own father had few reference points to guide him.

From London the tour moved to the United States and Europe, and in July we began a series of concerts in Israel and southern Africa. The latter was a first for most of the band members, who had no idea what to expect. As the plane prepared to land at Lobamba in Swaziland we caught our first view of the landscape, and as the band stepped from the plane on to African soil, drummer Steve Ferrone, who could always be relied on for a comedy moment, fell to his knees and kissed the ground saying, 'Rejoice, for your son has returned to the homeland!'

Having assumed we would play to a mixed crowd it was something of a surprise to find that the audience in Swaziland was predominantly white as thousands of South Africans, who were still living under the apartheid system, had crossed the border into Swaziland to see the show. While the international boycott of South Africa was enforced, South Africans were deprived of seeing international artists and jumped at this chance to see Eric. For the band, however, it was disturbing to be in Africa but playing to an all-white crowd.

While in Swaziland, Eric and the band were invited to take tea with King Mswati III. It was an honour to visit the palace and fraternise with royalty. The king, who by tradition had many wives, took quite a shine to the gorgeous Katie Kissoon, and the band teased her mercilessly about a potential marriage proposal and her future at the king's court.

From Swaziland we moved on to Harare in Zimbabwe where we performed two sell-out shows, again to white audiences. This was not at all what we'd expected. Perhaps Eric's music held little appeal for a black audience, or was the real issue that the ticket price was too high? The concerts in Gaborone and Botswana were the same. As always, the shows were fantastic and the audiences wildly appreciative, but the band were disappointed.

Our last stop on the tour was Maputo, in Mozambique. Mozambique was still suffering from the effects of a brutal civil war that had begun two years after its independence from the Portuguese in 1975. None of us had ever seen the kind of poverty we witnessed in Mozambique and were unaware that there was a degree of danger in us performing there. The conditions under which people lived were inhuman and the city slums shocked us to the core. Under Portuguese rule Maputo had once been an elegant city built for the privileged white few, with European-style buildings, tree-lined avenues and tram cars. We now witnessed the decaying grandeur of a former colonial power and the devastating aftermath of war.

Upon our arrival in Maputo we were met by Miss Nyeleti Mondlane, who ushered the band on to an awaiting bus. As we made our way through potholed streets to the Hotel Polana, an architectural jewel in Maputo's crown, Nyeleti treated us to a pocket-sized history of Mozambique. Everyone was highly impressed with this dynamo of a woman who was welcoming, charismatic and spoke English with an American accent.

As a telling reminder of the challenges Mozambicans faced, the usual chocolates left on the pillow of my hotel bed were replaced with a packet of condoms, an unequivocal statement about the HIV and AIDS epidemic throughout Africa. Gazing at the ocean while sipping tea in the lounge of the Hotel Polana, one could easily forget about the realities of life outside, and as a welcome breeze rustled the potted palms a tall man wearing a motorcycle helmet entered.

'Sorry I'm late,' said the man as he removed his helmet. 'My name is Eddie Mondlane, welcome to Mozambique. Are you all settling in OK?'

The brother of the dynamic lady we'd met on the bus earlier explained that he and his team were helping the British promoters put on the Maputo concert. He was striking looking, his head was shaved and he was wearing a sweatband.

'Hey Eddie, why are you wearing a headband?' asked the keyboard player, Alan.

With a flick of his head, he replied, 'It's to keep my long blond hair out of my eyes.'

I liked a man who didn't take himself too seriously. At that point the man in the headband had my full attention.

The concert at the Machava stadium in Maputo was to be the largest of Eric's African shows and the proceeds given to charities assisting the struggling nation. The tickets, priced at one dollar, made the concert accessible for all Mozambicans. On the day of

Eric Clapton, Katie Kissoon and Tessa, Maputo, Mozambique, 1989

the show, artists from South Africa, Zimbabwe and Mozambique performed from early morning in the blistering heat. The stadium was packed to the gills, and members of the Eric Clapton band were moved to tears as we stood on stage looking out over 70,000 people. Some in the crowd waved homemade banners. One read: 'Thank you Eric Clapton, you are bringing us one step closer to freedom'. Before our arrival we'd had no idea if Mozambicans knew who Eric Clapton was. Clearly they did, and loved the music. The concert was a resounding success and an emotional day for all of us.

After the show, as we made our way towards the bus waiting to take us back to the hotel, Eduardo, the intriguing guy with the headband, offered to carry my bag for me. I thanked him and he flashed me a smile as I passed it to him. Eduardo placed his hand over mine and held it there a little too long; long enough for me to feel the unexpected but exhilarating energy between us, and certainly long enough for the sleeping butterflies in my stomach to spring to life in a frenzy of activity. At a celebratory dinner that night I was seated disappointingly far from Eduardo, at the opposite end of the table. I so wanted to get to know him a little before we left the next day. Though I knew that I'd probably never see him again, I was inexplicably drawn to this man I'd met only two days earlier. Spirits were high, the band were elated and it was great to see Eric looking relaxed and happy, having truly enjoyed the concert. Over dinner we all spoke of the impact that Mozambique and its welcoming people had had on us. The following morning, happy to escape the blistering Maputo heat, the band sat in the ice-cold airport departure lounge. I hurriedly scribbled my phone number on a piece of paper and handed it to Eduardo's sister, Nyeleti. I knew next to nothing about this man, but there was no doubt in my mind that if given the chance I'd be happy to learn more.

In London, Duran Duran had re-formed after guitarist Andy and drummer Roger Taylor left. Andy was replaced by Warren Cuccurullo, a talented American guitarist and writer. I was invited to work on tracks for their sixth studio album, *Liberty*. I really liked Warren who, for me, brought renewed musical credibility to the band. Simon Le Bon, Nick Rhodes and John Taylor had always been recognised for their sartorial style and timeless pop songs, and the new tracks showed off their musical maturity. *Liberty* reached the Top Ten in the UK album charts.

As a kid I remember emulating the smoky vocal tones and the smoky eyes of soul singer Dusty Springfield. She was one of my mother Molly's favourites, and *Son of a Preacher Man* and Dusty's versions of Burt Bacharach songs like *Anyone Who Had a Heart* could be heard pulsing out of our record player on a Sunday morning. In the late 1970s and early 1980s she had released a string of overlooked albums. Dusty's new collaboration, *What*

Have I Done to Deserve This? produced by The Pet Shop Boys, had rightfully put her back on top again. It's hard to articulate the feeling of working with an artist you have grown up admiring. Throughout my childhood I spent hours dreaming about meeting singers like Dusty. She was a British legend and I was particularly thrilled when Neil and Chris asked me to work on *I Want to Stay Here* for her album *Reputation*. Neil shared with me how insecure Dusty felt about her vocal abilities, and how she needed reassurance. This was no difficulty as she'd always had an instantly recognisable voice that had not diminished over the years. I was – and remain – a huge Dusty Springfield fan, and consider her to be one of the United Kingdom's finest soul singers. *Reputation* became her bestselling album in Britain since the 1970s.

The key to success as a session singer was understanding where you fitted in. If the spotlight beckoned, you were better off making the move towards your goals without delay, for session singing could become quicksand. The longer you focused on someone else's journey, the longer it would take to achieve your dreams. Stardom won't wait.

On a morning in September 1989 I received an unexpected phone call that would alter the course of my life.

'Hey, how are you?' said the male caller. 'Can you guess who this is?'

As I tried desperately to recall where I had heard this rich voice before, we chatted comfortably until it finally hit me who it was. It was the man I hadn't expected to hear from again.

'I'm here on business, would you like to join me for dinner tonight?' said Eduardo.

I responded as calmly as I was able, which wasn't even close to sounding casual.

'Yes, that would be great, thanks, I'd love to.'

'Great, how about 7.30pm? I'm staying at the Hilton Hotel on Park Lane.'

Once again, this man that I barely knew had managed to unleash my butterflies.

Despite declarations about my independence and relief at being an unattached female, since returning from Mozambique I hadn't been able to stop thinking about Eduardo. As I drove towards the Hilton that evening my stomach flipped with nerves and the irony that Eduardo was staying in the same hotel where Richard and I had had our first date. I knew nothing about this person met briefly on a three-day trip to Mozambique, and not having been on a date in ten years, hoped fervently I could stay calm and collected.

As Eduardo opened his hotel room door, I was surprised. Dressed in a T-shirt and loose cotton pants he looked deliciously handsome, and trimmer than I remembered.

'Come on in, Miss Niles,' he said revealing a set of perfect teeth.

How could I have missed those in Mozambique? Maybe we'd never been this close to each other before.

With vintage champagne, far-reaching views over Hyde Park and music that was the right side of cool, the evening was off to a great start.

We talked easily about ourselves for what seemed like hours, and later during dinner at Mr Chow's it began to dawn on me that it was going to be hard to extricate myself from this fascinating man. Eduardo was charming, charismatic and intelligent, but before I had the chance to lose my bearings he let slip the crushing news that he was married. My heart sank. I had not left a distressed marriage only to jump into a damaging and, as far as I could see, futureless relationship with Eduardo. I drove home that night with a powerful mix of emotions running through my head. I was undeniably attracted to this man and wanted to spend time getting to know him, but there were obvious dangers. Eduardo was the kind of man who could break down all my defences and resolves, something I had never experienced before, and my recently reconstructed life was in danger of being swiftly and expertly thrown off course.

The career of Oleta Adams was taking off and, after her supporting role with Tears for Fears, she was about to record her own album. Roland Orzabal, who co-produced the tracks, brought a uniquely British slant to Oleta's music; had the tracks been recorded in America, they would have had a quite different flavour. Roland's vision for Oleta was not a conventional R&B album. *Circle of One* showcased her extraordinary musicianship and song-writing capabilities infused with blues, soul, gospel and pop. The single *Rhythm of Life* was in classic Tears for Fears mould, whereas the autobiographical *I've Got to Sing My Song*, a piano-based ballad, showed off Oleta's exquisite voice. Listening to her performance in the studio it was impossible not to be moved to tears by her beautiful vocals and profound sincerity. I was also in precisely the emotional place for her music to touch me. My new feelings felt both uncomfortable and thrilling, and over the coming months I was to discover that the laws of attraction and love defy all rules.

Early in 1990 the Eric Clapton band returned to The Albert Hall for a record-breaking season of 18 shows. Divided into different instrumental formats, the performances featured a four-piece blues band, a nine-piece band and the nine-piece band together with The National Philharmonic Orchestra conducted by composer Michael Kamen, a long-time friend of Eric. Additional dates at The Albert Hall were added in 1991 and culminated in the release of Eric's *24 Nights* CD.

His relationship with Lory Del Santo now over, Eric began a relationship with model Carla Bruni. He seemed infatuated with her and she came to many of his shows that year but it was not to end well.

'So I told Mick,' said Eric, recalling the warning he had given to his famous Lothario friend at a party he was attending with Carla. 'Listen, I'm serious about this one so just leave her alone, OK? I know you, don't even think about it.'

But Mick Jagger and Carla Bruni had other ideas however, and began a much-publicised affair.

On 30 June 1990, Eric and an all-star band featuring Elton John and Mark Knopfler performed an outdoor show in the grounds of Knebworth House, a major venue for pop and rock concerts. The boys in the band sported Versace suits in an array of pastel colours and Katie and I decided to wear hats. Unfortunately these proved problematic due to the weather conditions that day, and during *Tearing Us Apart* I spent most of the song trying to prevent my hat from blowing away into the crowd.

The Eric Clapton All Star Band at Knebworth, 1990, (L to R) Nathan East, Tessa Niles, Steve Ferrone, Guy Fletcher, Ray Cooper, Mark Knopfler, John Illsley, Eric Clapton, Alan Clark, Phil Palmer, Greg Phillanganes, Elton John and Katie Kissoon (Photograph courtesy of Brian Aris).

Despite attempts to end the unlooked-for and unexpected relationship with Eduardo, I found myself falling more deeply in love with him. Both of us battled with our feelings, and although we knew we should not be involved with each other, it was not enough to halt us. I would never have asked Eduardo to leave his marriage, but he'd arrived at the point where he felt he could no longer continue and made the painful decision to move to London to be with me. It was unimaginably hard for Eduardo's wife and family to deal with the break-up, and the early years of our relationship were fraught with acrimony. Eduardo's two children, Kristofer and Alessia, were caught in the middle, of course. I badly wanted to forge a healthy relationship with them but knew it would take time and patience for them to trust their father's new partner.

Eduardo Mondlane Junior was the product of black and white parents who had met at a Christian summer camp in the United States in the 1950s. His mother, Janet, was only 16 when introduced to Eduardo Senior, a counsellor at the camp. Older than Janet by 14 years, Eduardo Senior was born in Mozambique in 1920, the son of a chief in Nwadjahane, a village three hours' drive north of the capital, then known as Lourenço Marques (LM). Under colonial rule since the 16th century, the indigenous people of Portuguese East Africa were prohibited from receiving an education past fourth grade and Eduardo found employment as a 'house boy' for a missionary and his family living in LM. Recognising the young man's intelligence and hunger for learning, the missionary, Andre Clerc, became Eduardo's mentor and provided the opportunity for him to attend a Swiss mission school. Eduardo thrived there, and with the help of scholarships in Portugal, South Africa and America, where he obtained a degree in Anthropology and Sociology, went on to become the first black PhD in the history of his country. His subsequent marriage to Janet in 1950s America caused outrage at a time when interracial relationships were taboo.

In 1957 Eduardo Senior became a United Nations official, but resigned later the same year to participate in political activism. The couple moved from the United States to Tanzania, where

Janet and Eduardo Mondlane Sr, Evanston, Illinois, 1954.

Eduardo led the Mozambican liberation struggle. Having achieved independence in 1961, Tanzania was receptive to the cries for help from other countries in the region that were still suffering from colonial oppression. Eduardo and Janet had three children: Eduardo Junior, Jennifer and Nyeleti. From 1962 Eduardo Senior served as founder and President of the Mozambican Liberation Front (FRELIMO), but before his dream of Mozambican independence could be realised he was assassinated on 3 February 1969 by a parcel bomb, mailed to him in a book. Mozambique finally achieved independence from Portugal in 1975.

My Eduardo's childhood had therefore been exceptionally difficult. True, he was the son of a great man, but Eduardo Senior's political career meant that his son had grown up with a largely absent father. After his father's death, Eduardo was sent away to be educated in Russia, a difficult period for him, not only because of the isolation he felt but also because having to study in Russian was no picnic. Eddie and I would talk for hours, sharing stories of our past and dreams for the future. He opened up to me about his life, and we shared a passion for music. He had run a music production company when he lived in Mozambique, hence his involvement with the Eric Clapton concert. Though now involved in business, he fully understood the music industry and supported me in everything I did. We made the decision not to spend long periods apart from each other as we both knew what the consequences would be if we did. Eduardo and I both felt the need to stay connected despite the occupational necessity of having to spend time apart. Well aware of the perils of developing a separate life on the road, I was determined not to repeat previous mistakes.

Tessa and Eduardo Mondlane Jr, Tokyo Station, Japan, 1990.

In 1990 the Eric Clapton *Journeyman* tour continued to perform to sell-out crowds across the United States. Upon arrival at The Four Seasons in Chicago, the band was informed that the next two shows would take place at the Alpine Music Valley Theatre in the town of East Troy, Wisconsin, a two-hour drive from Chicago, and would travel to the outdoor shows via helicopter instead of our usual private jet.

'I'm not sure how I feel about this, are you Katie? I mean, I've travelled by helicopter before but I'm not 100 per cent comfortable with it.'

'I'm really not sure either but I do get that it's gonna be much quicker this way,' said a decidedly unconvinced Katie. 'I just hope it's safe.'

We both felt uncomfortable with this mode of transport as we took off for the first of the two gigs at Alpine Valley. But 20 minutes later, back on terra firma, all thoughts turned to the sound check for the show. Later that night Stevie Ray Vaughan, the legendary blues guitarist, supported Eric on stage and his playing was electrifying. Also performing with us were Buddy Guy and

Robert Cray, a blues dream team if ever there was one. After the show the EC band flew back to Chicago in four helicopters, an even more unnerving experience at night, and on landing at the heliport we were met by the usual fleet of black limousines and driven back to our hotel.

The following afternoon the band again travelled to the Alpine Valley Theatre by helicopter.

At the airport Nathan East announced, 'Greg and I are not going to be joining you today. A friend of mine has a plane and has offered to fly us both to the outdoor show.'

Nathan, a flight enthusiast, jumped at his friend's offer although it was very unusual for the band not to travel together.

'So we'll see you cats on the other side. Try not to miss us too much.'

That night the concert was again phenomenal, with the sound of searing blues guitars audible for miles around. The exhilarated musicians left the stage just after midnight and because Nathan and Greg returned to Chicago in their friend's plane there were extra seats available in the helicopters. As Katie and I sat inside one of the four awaiting choppers, the pilot's radio crackled that the weather conditions were worsening and we should make haste and leave.

'Stevie, you jump in this one with Tess and Katie,' shouted tour manager Pete Jackson, as he listened intently to the two-way radio. Stevie clambered in between Katie and me wearing his signature bandana, elated from the performance.

'Actually no, scratch that, can you go in the one behind?' said Peter, struggling to be heard above the noise of the rotor blades.

'Sorry ladies,' said Stevie as he climbed out of the chopper. 'Looks like I won't be having the pleasure of your company this evening. See you back at the hotel.'

Unlike the first night, the weather was not good; thick fog enveloped the area and heavy dew had settled on the windscreen. The choppers took off at two-minute intervals, and Katie and I were hugely relieved when, 20 minutes later, we could make out the lights of the Chicago runway ahead. As they had the previous night, the limousines whisked us back to the comfort of the hotel.

Back in my room, I telephoned Eduardo who had been concerned about us being transported to the gig by helicopter, a mode of transport he felt was ill-advised. At the time, he was working on a project with the Boeing organisation and knew a great deal about all types of aircraft. I told him about the weather conditions but assured him that all was fine. I fell into a deep sleep but was startled awake in the early hours of the morning by the phone ringing.

Fumbling for the receiver, I answered and the woman's voice at the other end simply repeated, 'Thank God, oh thank God you're OK... Tess, you're OK.'

Heavy with sleep, it took a few moments before I recognised the voice of Dolette.

'Of course I'm OK,' I replied, 'why wouldn't I be? Dolette, what's happened?'

Dolette's voice was shaking. 'I was driving along the highway and they announced on the radio that members of Eric Clapton's band have been killed in a helicopter crash.'

'What? No, it's not true,' I protested. 'I would know about it, I would have been told.'

'OK, OK honey,' Dolette replied. 'I'm going to let you go now, you need to find out what's going on. I'm just so relieved you're OK. I'll call you later, love you.'

I sat motionless as my friend's words began to sink in. Could somebody be playing a sick joke? Surely I'd have been told if anything serious had happened. Had Eric been killed? If there were six people dead then it had to be members of the band. As I got out of bed and opened the curtains I looked around the room. Blinking in the brightness, my eyes were drawn to the door and what looked like a doormat made of white paper on the plush red carpet. Frozen to the spot, I felt the blood pounding in my ears as I realised that this was no mat in front of me but individual handwritten notes. My legs buckled beneath me and I knew at that moment something terrible had happened. I crawled to the phone and dialled Roger Forrester, who told me everything.

The helicopter accident had killed agent Bobby Brooks, Stevie Ray Vaughan, pilot Jeff Brown, assistant tour manager Colin Smythe and Eric's bodyguard, Nigel Browne. All were killed instantly when helicopter number four ploughed into the side of a man-made ski slope next to the Alpine Valley venue. It took time for rescuers to find the wreckage, as there had been no fire or explosion. Shocked and tearful, I managed to speak to Eduardo and let him know the news. Eduardo's worst fears had been realised, fears that he had expressed to me only a few hours before. I spoke to my brother Ian, who had heard Sky News reporting that six members of the Clapton band had been killed, and was able to reassure him and my parents that I was fine, but in truth I was in a state of shock. Later that morning Eric and Stevie's brother, Jimmie Vaughan, were summoned by the Walworth County coroner to identify the bodies.

United in shock and sadness, Eric and the band expressed their grief in different ways. Some were quiet; others allowed the unpredictable waves of emotion to wash over them. All of us were confused and some were angry. It helped to be together, and when one of us crumpled under the weight of the tragedy we picked them up and held them. Far from home and our loved ones, we clung to each other for the support that helped us through those dark hours after the accident.

With the three last dates of the tour still to perform there were decisions to be made. With the whole band assembled the next day, Eric calmly addressed us.

'This is the question that I wanted to put to all of you as I feel it's not really just my decision to make. Do you want to carry on and do the last shows or do you think we should cancel them?'

Eric's face was etched with pain as he listened to his band; I was touched at his concern for our feelings but the response was divided. I felt uncomfortable at having to perform through my grief and didn't think I'd be able to do it; others felt that show-biz tradition demanded that the show must go on. Our emotions were still raw, but the decision was taken to perform the last three shows and complete the tour.

'OK,' said Eric, nodding in acceptance. 'We do this for Stevie and Bobby and Nigel and Colin.'

With heavy hearts we faced the absence of our much-loved colleagues and, looking back, this was the right decision. Working on the shows focused our attention away from ourselves and united us in something greater. Time, and in our case music, helped to heal the wounds.

CHAPTER SIX

Tears and fears

The major part of 1990 having been spent on the road, settling back into home life after the accident was not easy. I missed the people with whom I had become inextricably linked through our shared loss. As life eventually took on a new shape, on 27 January 1991 I celebrated my 30th birthday, with Eduardo. He and I grew ever closer and I learned increasingly to trust his judgment. Studio work kept me busy between tours with Eric. Singer Sonia Jones and I collaborated on a track for The Rolling Stones – or 'The Strolling Bones' as Eduardo liked to call them. The live album, *Flashpoint*, was recorded while the Stones were on their massive *Steel Wheels/Urban Jungle* tour, and released in 1991.

Months before, during a break in the *Journeyman* tour, Sonia and I had worked on the song *Sex Drive*, one of two studio tracks recorded for the album. These recordings were to be the last for bassist and founding Stones member Bill Wyman. In the studio Mick Jigger was as animated as he was on stage, strutting and dancing around the control room as only he can. At the time, Mick was still seeing Eric's ex, Carla Bruni, and seemed to have an extra spring in his step. Carla posed an intoxicating challenge for him: she was young, beautiful, and had her own money. Eric was still smarting from his unceremonious break-up from her, but Carla was strategically working her way through the world's rich and famous in her unceasing quest for a man with even greater power, a quest that would eventually lead her to the arms of the most powerful man in France.

On 20 March 1991 the news flashed around the world that Eric Clapton's young son, Conor, had died tragically after falling from a window of a New York apartment building. The accident happened when his mother, Lory Del Santo, took Conor to New York to visit Eric. The boy fell from a 53rd-floor apartment in a Manhattan building his mother and her boyfriend were renting. A housekeeper had removed a window to clean it and there was no window guard to protect the four-year-old, who was killed instantly. Lory and Eric were no longer together and although Eric had not been actively involved in his son's life, at the time of the accident he had been trying to build a closer relationship with him and would now never have the opportunity. Devastated at the news, the first thoughts of the band, management and crew were for Eric. Conor was his only son.

The funeral was a bleak affair held in Surrey at St Mary Magdalene Church, Ripley, Eric's home town. Walls of reporters and journalists gathered outside the churchyard. Eric was stoic but clearly a broken man, and the sight of him watching as his son's tiny coffin was lowered into the ground was unbearable. Conor's unnatural death was impossible to reconcile. At the graveside, Lory and her mother clung to each other in their grief.

At the reception afterwards the small gathering of Eric's closest friends and family stood about solemnly, drinking sweet tea. As I chatted with George Harrison and Patti Boyd I wondered if Eric would have the strength to survive this second dark period.

Later that year rehearsals began at Bray Studios, a film and television facility near Maidenhead. George Harrison was persuaded by Eric to join him on a tour of Japan, and George agreed that after Eric's recent tragedy it would be therapeutic for both of them to get back on the road. He was reticent, however, about performing live. His voice had blown on his Dark Horse Tour of 1974, leaving him insecure about his vocal capabilities. From day one of rehearsals at Bray Studios, Katie and I reassured George that we and the entire band were there to provide all the vocal help he needed. Apart from Eric, Nathan, Greg and Chuck, who were all great vocalists, we were joined by a new singer/guitar player and all-round nice guy, Andy Fairweather Low. With more than enough singers to support George, the rehearsals came together easily. George was sweet, generous and always funny. He'd arrive at rehearsals with flowers, and on one occasion ordered a cake from the company of his old friend, Jane Asher. The cake, a huge replica of the stage set complete with detailed marzipan figures of each musician, was immediately given pride of place in front of the stage. On closer inspection, Andy, a blue-eyed Welshman, was found to have been made from black marzipan, resulting in his new nickname, BB Fairweather Low.

Everyone wanted to please George. His charm and fun-loving nature was in stark contrast to Eric, who seemed introverted and withdrawn, still hurting from Conor's death. Friends and family including Ringo Starr, Jimmy Nail and Phil Collins came down to the studios for a private performance of the show shortly before we left for Japan. The set included music from The Beatles years and solo numbers from George and Eric. George's voice was in good shape and his confidence had grown over the course of the rehearsals. It was such a blast performing Beatles tunes. *If I Needed Someone, Something* and my favourite, *Taxman*, sounded amazing. George added new lyrics to *Taxman* to update it: instead of the original 'Ah, ah, Mr Wilson' background vocals we sang, 'Ah, ah, Boris Yeltsin.'

Eric had for years had a love-affair with Italian fashion designers, and worn Gianni Versace outfits on stage. For The Rock Legends Tour of Japan he chose Giorgio Armani, and the band was ushered off to the Armani store in Bond Street to be kitted out. Eric had suggested that we all wear suits and the guys looked amazing in theirs, but despite the exquisite tailoring Katie and I looked frumpy in our pinstripe numbers worn with striped shirts done up at the collar.

*Katie and Tessa wearing Armani on the Eric
Clapton/George Harrison Tour of Japan, 1991.*

'Is that what you're wearing?' said George with a smirk. 'Well it's an interesting look I suppose. You remind me of airline stewardesses.'

Not exactly the rock 'n' roll edge we were hoping for.

The press was out in force for our arrival at Tokyo's Narita airport. The last time George had been to Japan was with The Beatles in 1966. Back then, the band had been confined to their hotel under police protection and left it only under escort to perform their show. A militant organisation had made public threats against The Beatles, viewing their performance at the Budokan Hall as contrary to Japanese culture. When we arrived 25 years later, George was swamped by media representatives deprived of seeing him for a generation and considerably less attention was focused on Eric, who performed in Japan every year. It was difficult to tell if Eric was relieved or miffed at his unhindered passage through the airport.

Eric Clapton with Tessa and George Harrison at a band dinner, Capitol Tokyo Hotel, 1991.

George Harrison and Chuck Leavell, Capitol Tokyo Hotel, 1991.

The first of the seven Rock Legends shows was in the city of Yokohama. We travelled to most of the gigs via Japan's high-speed bullet train. At Tokyo station the local branch of the Hare Krishna movement and a small group of devotees, who had heard that George would be travelling by train, appeared on the platform to hand him gifts and food through the window. The show in Yokohama was a resounding success.

The band sounded incredible and George, still nervous, gave a masterful performance. The following day as the band gathered in the lobby of the hotel, we were surprised to see Eric's ex, Lory. As far as we knew, she and Eric were not seeing each other and it soon became clear that Eric was not at all happy about her being there. Roger, Eric's manager, confided that Lory had paid her own way to Japan but that Eric wanted nothing to do with her. Perhaps she was there with the intention of rekindling her relationship with him, but from Eric's attitude I couldn't see how this would happen. My heart went out to Lory. After the terrible loss of Conor she appeared desperately sad. Perhaps to cover her disappointment at Eric's coldness towards her she was flirtatious with the boys in the band, and looking back, it was possible that she felt comfortable in the company of the musicians who had shared the loss of her child with her.

The Rock Legends Tour rolled on, thrilling crowds who were treated to Eric's classic hits and George's well-loved solo and Beatles tunes. In spite of the uncomfortable relationship between Eric and Lory, she continued to travel with us. It seemed unfathomable that she would want to stay around, but maybe she was still seeking answers as to why Eric had locked her out of his life.

On our day off in the city of Hiroshima, George organised a party of us to visit the Peace Park, a memorial to the first city in the world to suffer a nuclear attack. We visited the museum, which was a sobering history lesson, and then spent time in the park where we took photos of George clowning around inside the giant peace bell. Eric did not come with us; still deeply affected by his son's death, he may have wanted to avoid further sadness. Years later, Lory revealed that she'd had a brief affair with George in Hiroshima; an attempt, maybe, to get back at Eric for his coldness towards her, or simply to alleviate her own unhappiness. She appeared to be seeking answers to and validation for her loss. I couldn't help but feel disappointed in George, but who was I to judge? This was rock 'n' roll.

Eduardo and I longed to escape city life in England and found a beautiful home in the quintessentially English village of Great Missenden. The village had a church, a pub and a post office and really not much else. We rented a sprawling Georgian house set in 70 acres of paddock and woodland where Benjamin Disraeli, prime minister to Queen Victoria, had once lived. The place was large enough for at least three families with its nine bedrooms, stables and outbuildings. I absolutely loved the house, and when not on the road with Eric, threw myself into being the lady of the manor. Clad in wellies and quilted jacket I grew vegetables and shopped for antiques and organic food. Talk about 'to the manor born!' Eduardo and I entertained a great deal and friends and family visited regularly. One New Year's Eve we hosted an extravagant party complete with caterers, floral designers, butlers, valet parking, ice sculptures, a Scottish piper and a celebrity magician.

Eduardo's mother, Janet, came from Mozambique to visit her son and his new partner. She was cool and understandably unsure of me in the beginning, but this gradually changed as we spent time together. Eduardo's children, Kristofer and Alessia, came over from the United States to spend their school summer holidays with us. They had only ever experienced living in apartments, so at first it was hard for them to adjust to our huge and scary house. From the beginning of my relationship with Eduardo he had explained that his children were his main priority, and this was one of the reasons I cared for him so deeply. I loved the fact that Eduardo loved his kids and was actively involved in their lives. Despite the distance that separated them he was a vigilant and caring father, visiting them every six weeks in New York and having them visit us at every opportunity.

The break-up between Eduardo and his wife was undeniably strained, and initially it was difficult for the children to adjust to their father's new life and new partner. I'd had no previous experience with children as there were none in my family while I grew up. I discovered that there is nothing instinctive about being a step-parent; I really wanted to be a good one, but it's a job you have to learn by doing it. Eduardo was patient and understanding, and Kris and Alessia were wonderful children. Young enough to adapt to their new situation, these two little bubble-haired, Italian-speaking people were not hard to love. Kris, intelligent and inquisitive by nature, and Alessia, with her sweet and caring disposition, slowly began to adjust to life in their new blended family.

Eric and the band returned to Bray Film Studios to rehearse for the MTV show Unplugged. This popular television series featured well-known artists performing acoustic versions of their hits. The band were to play a mix of Eric's favourite blues tunes, classics and new material he had written as a way of coming to terms with Conor's death. On the first day of rehearsals, Steve, Nathan, Andy, Ray, Chuck, Katie, Eric and I sat in a circle on the stage.

Eric began, 'So guys, I want to play you some of the new songs. I... I hope I can get through them. This first one's called *Tears in Heaven*.'

No one in the room was remotely prepared for what we heard that day. Listening to Eric was like looking at an open wound: his pain and loss were palpable. The heart-breaking ballad captured the essence of Eric's grief, with its deeply personal plea: 'Would you know my name, if I saw you in Heaven?' None of us thought we were capable of performing the song without breaking down every time. Not for the first time I marvelled at Eric's strength. His ability to pour his grief into his music stunned us into the realisation that if he could perform the set he had in mind, then so could we. Andy Fairweather Low had done a terrific job of stripping the songs down and re-arranging them, but every member of the band was faced with an additional musical challenge: performing acoustically required an approach adapted to suit the needs of a quieter, more sensitive format.

The classic, *Layla*, was given an unexpected new twist by Eric. Who would have thought that this driving rock song could be re-interpreted as an acoustic blues number? My personal favourite was a song that was not included on the *Unplugged* album.

'This one's called *Circus Left Town*,' said Eric softly. 'We had spent the day together... I'd taken the boy to the circus the day before the accident.'

Once again the band were speechless. Eric's performance was profoundly moving and showed his storytelling at its finest. *Unplugged* was performed to an audience of only 300 in a small and intimate setting that was perfect for the occasion. Each of us in the band felt Eric's pain and understood deeply the importance of him being able to express his grief through music, but at the time we had no idea of the impact these recordings would have. When released, the *Unplugged* album reached number one in the United States and earned no fewer than six Grammy Awards for Eric, three of them for *Tears in Heaven*. To date, *Unplugged* remains his best-selling album.

'Your dad's been taken to hospital,' announced Molly's shaky voice down the phone.

'Oh no, Mum, what do they think's wrong with him?'

'The doctors aren't sure yet. I found him doubled over in pain on the living room floor so I called an ambulance. They suspect it might be something called pancreatitis. He's not in pain and says he's comfortable.'

'I've no idea what that is. Is it serious?' I said, unable to hide my concern.

'Well, no one really knows yet, we're just waiting to hear more from the doctors. It just all happened so quickly.' Her voice sounded small and fearful.

'Are you all right mum?'

'Yes, I'm OK, I'm just not used to your dad being sick.'

'Try not to worry too much, he's in the right place now. I'll be down tomorrow.'

Until then my father had been an active 73-year-old with no health concerns. After weeks of testing he was eventually diagnosed with pancreatitis, a virus causing severe inflammation of the pancreas. My family were told very little about his condition. His doctors let us know he was stable, although his recovery would take some time, but at no point during his illness were we advised that pancreatitis could be life-threatening.

I began rehearsals with George Harrison for a benefit concert at The Albert Hall. The show was in aid of the Natural Law Party, a transnational political party founded in 1992 on the principles of Transcendental Meditation, the laws of nature and their application to all levels of government. Since the 1960s and The Beatles' well-publicised relationship with Maharishi Mahesh Yogi, George had been a powerful proponent of eastern spirituality and Transcendental Meditation. Joining George on stage for the performance were Gary Moore, Ringo Starr and Joe Walsh. The all-star band included Will Lee, Steve Ferrone, Greg Phillanganes, Katie Kissoon, Chuck Leavell, Ray Cooper and Mike Campbell. As far as I know the show was not filmed or recorded, but apparently bootleg copies exist. George saw humour in everything and his infectious wit attracted people to him, but he also possessed a questioning nature and could be sharply cynical about things that did not feel authentic. He was generous and had the ability to make everyone who worked with him feel valued. The concert at The Albert Hall was outstanding. The London audience felt especially lucky as they had not been treated to a live perform-ance from George in many years. As always for me, it was a truly special time working with him and I adored George's wife Olivia and son Dhani, whom I'd got to know while on tour in Japan. After the concert I arrived back late at the house, adrenalin still pumping from the performance, and had difficulty falling asleep as the show re-ran in my head. In the early hours of the following morning my world collapsed as I was awoken with the news that my father had died.

While I was performing with George at the Natural Law Party concert, my father's condition had worsened. My brother Ian was at the hospital with our mother, Molly, who was advised to go home and get some sleep. Only then did the doctors discuss with Ian how gravely ill our father was. As our father grew pro-gressively weaker, Ian stayed at his side, and in the early hours of the morning, with Ian holding his hand, he died. I was shocked beyond belief at the news, as were all the family. Later that morn-ing, I drove down to my parents' home and helped set the plans for my father's funeral in motion. Molly was in a state of disbe-lief but quietly went about the business of informing family and friends. My sweet, placid, even-tempered father, Leonard Francis Webb, had always encouraged me to follow my dreams. A kind, steadfast man and loving parent, he had allowed me to be exactly what I wanted to be.

Session work continued to flow in including a chance to work on my third project with Duran Duran, who were recording tracks for an album titled *The Wedding Album*. On arrival at guitar player Warren's house for the evening session, I found his living room had become a makeshift recording room decorated with candles, lava lamps and rock 'n' roll ephemera, an appropriate atmosphere for the track I was there to work on. *Come Undone* featured a sexy, trance-like groove. Warren played the hypnotic guitar-riff on the intro and Simon Le Bon sang the song, written for his wife Yasmin. I added lead vocals on the bridge section. 'Can't ever keep from falling apart at the seams, cannot believe you're tearing my heart to pieces,' my plaintive answer to Simon's call.

'Oh my God, Warren. You've got me singing at the top of my range here,' I protested after a few run-throughs. 'Let me try it in a breathy voice.'

'Sure, give it a go. But you're not supposed to be too nice sounding,' Warren's voice directed through the headphones.

The tape rolled and I tried it again.

Nick Rhodes interjected

'Erm, it's not exactly right yet, Tess. It just sounds too soft and light. I don't know, try something else, full voice maybe.'

'Really, you're sure about that? Do I have permission to unleash the inner diva?'

'Absolutely... go for it.'

Warren and Nick wanted the edgier sound that I got when the notes were pushed, so I did exactly that and they were happy. I love the song and to this day it remains my favourite Duran track. *Come Undone* was released as the second single after their smash hit *Ordinary World*. *The Wedding Album* re-established the band's commercial and critical success and went multi-platinum in the US and Canada.

It was great to be associated with continued hit singles and albums as their sleeve notes provided invaluable publicity for me – the best way for other producers and industry people to see my current credits. As in other industries, you are only as good as your last success. Thankfully I was still in demand as a studio singer, and between touring, recording sessions and TV and radio commercials, was continuously working. Advertising sessions could be challenging. Attempting to interpret a non-musician's ideas for a product could test one to the limit. Once, when working on a job for Kinder chocolate and trying to fulfil the brief to 'sound like a turtle', the advertising executive asked, 'Could you perhaps make what you are singing sound a bit more green?' What do you say to something like that? But the beauty of advertising and voiceover work was that it was usually quick, and the subsequent repeat fees lucrative. Under those conditions I was prepared to be any creature, with any coloured voice.

An opportunity to record with The Pet Shop Boys was always a treat. The duo were busy in the studio recording their fifth album. Nearly two and a half years since their last one, *Very* was considered to be a turning point that showcased their shift from electronic pop to richly instrumented dance arrangements, and when Neil Tennant publicly disclosed his much-debated homosexuality, it became the title of the 'coming out' album.

Shortly after the sessions for *Very* I returned to work with the boys on a track in aid of Comic Relief. The song, *Absolutely Fabulous*, was based on the BBC comedy of the same name and featured dialogue taken from the popular show. The Pet Shop Boys liked working out of Sarm Studios. Owned by my good friend Trevor Horn, it was the studio of choice for many successful bands. The Tom Jones single *If You Only Knew*, from the album *The Lead and How to Swing It*, was recorded at Sarm with Trevor producing and a choir of singers on background vocals, including me. To use a choir on a session was expensive, but sometimes the track cried out for that kind of vocal magnificence and it was fun to work with a number of accomplished singers when my work usually involved singing on my own, or with one or two others.

During the summer of 1994, I flew down to the south of France with Duran Duran to work on my fourth album project with them. *Thank You* was an album of cover songs. I sang on Duran's interpretation of Elvis Costello's *Watching the Detectives* and the single, *Perfect Day*, written by Lou Reed. The boys had rented a grand house in Cannes for the summer and turned it into a temporary recording studio. In the elegantly decorated rooms, state-of-the-art recording equipment nestled comfortably between the 17th-century antiques. Lunch breaks were taken by the sparkling pool with its views of the Mediterranean. Duran Duran never slummed it.

Later in the year I began work with the alternative rock band Suede. Their *Dog Man Star* album reached number three in the UK album chart and is considered their masterpiece. Suede became known as 'the unwitting inventors of Britpop'. Working in this genre was a different experience for me. On the sessions the lead singer, Brett Anderson, was sullen and appeared singularly unimpressed by having a female singer in the studio. My suggestions of vocal ideas were met with indifference. Later I was told that Brett and guitarist Bernard Butler were having serious problems, which culminated in Butler exiting the band before the album was completed. Maybe this accounted for Brett's seeming lack of interest. It was a tough session for me, quite different from the light-hearted but focused pop sessions I was used to.

On my travels I'd often encounter aspiring singers who would seek advice about how to become successful. So many of them, when asked what they would like to achieve, expressed a wish to be famous. This always stunned me. I view fame as a by-product of hard work and determination, rather than the ultimate goal. Of itself, fame is transient and not enough to sustain a career. Young people are sold the distorted idea of achieving celebrity without content, and with so many television shows documenting a swift rise to celebrity this gives young performers the impression that with very little experience they can become successful. Success is almost always a combination of talent, study, persistence, hard work, luck, and timing.

Unless you understand that music careers are built over many years, you are likely to be disappointed. The artists that least realise the work it takes, those that achieve instant fame, are generally unprepared for what fame brings. The younger a person is, the harder it is for them to deal with the challenges. On too many occasions we see young lives playing out in front of the camera, watching every mistake amplified and every aspect of their lives discussed ad nauseam. Make no mistake, without guidance or mentorship the train will go off the rails.

Tessa, 1994

My association with the actor and singer Jimmy Nail began in 1986 when I sang on his single *That's the Way Love Is*. Jimmy rose to fame when he portrayed Oz, the much-loved character in the TV series *Auf Wiedersehen Pet*. With his unusual looks, haunting voice and startlingly honest acting, Jimmy became hugely popular. Six feet three inches tall, this Newcastle native cut a striking figure, and crossed successfully to the music business while continuing his acting career. I loved Jimmy and was drawn to his tough, no bullshit approach to life. We crossed paths again in 1995, when he asked me to join his Summer Strummer Tour. The band comprised excellent musicians, including my great friend Andy Caine on guitar and vocals. Also in the band, I was introduced to keyboard player and writer Guy Chambers, who was to become influential in my career.

Duran Duran had successfully negotiated many pitfalls on their road to success and had maintained their popularity. In March I flew with the band to New York to perform at the opening of The Fashion Cafe. This restaurant concept was initially fronted by supermodels Claudia Schiffer, Naomi Campbell, Elle Macpherson and Christy Turlington, but I thought the idea of an eatery involving super-skinny models a contradiction in terms. Everyone knows that models live on cigarettes and coffee, but at the time the venture was hailed as 'the next big thing'.

New York had always held great appeal for me. I love the energy, the architecture, the frantic pace and, of course, the shopping – ohhh God, the shopping! Duran always stayed in the best hotels, close to the trendy stores and restaurants, so one never needed to travel far to indulge in New York's finest food and retail therapy. No problem there, I've always had a shoe fetish (thanks Mrs Hughes).

For our US outing Duran hired a designer in London to create some frocks for me. Duran's sense of style and clear understanding of the link between fashion, art and music had always set them apart from other bands. The opening night at The Fashion Cafe was a glittering affair: wall-to-wall paparazzi, New York's most beautiful people, celebrities and wannabes, with entertainment provided by the ultimate party band. Duran Duran were fabulous and had the entire restaurant on its well-heeled feet rocking to *Rio, Wild Boys, Hungry like the Wolf* and *The Reflex.* Oddly though, considering it was the opening of a new eatery, I remember nothing about the actual food.

From New York we flew to Las Vegas, Nevada, to perform at the grand opening of the world's first Hard Rock Hotel. From its giant neon signs, decadent decor, casinos and clubs with names like Rehab and The Joint, to its legendary collection of music memorabilia, the hotel pays homage to all things rock 'n' roll: a veritable paradise for sinners and music-lovers alike. Written above the main entrance are Stevie Ray Vaughan's prophetic words: 'When this house is rocking, don't bother knocking, come on in.' The opening night party was nothing less than insane, and the band's performance amazing. It was a hot, sweaty mess on stage and the Duran boys wore more 'guy liner' than I did. The crowd went wild for the show and there were several different party invitations to choose from afterwards. But here's where it got tricky. I remember travelling from the hotel to a party and someone pouring me a vodka and tonic in the car. After that, I don't remember much other than getting back to my room in the early hours and the crippling hangover I woke up with the next morning. Always mindful of remaining professional, my guess is that someone slipped me a mickey that night. I was totally and utterly incapacitated the following day, barely able to lift my head from the pillow, and missed my flight back to London. I was mortified, thinking that I might have disgraced myself somehow. However, no one seemed to think anything of it, and my behaviour was probably tame compared with that of the experienced party animals I was with.

Background vocalists know only too well that their reputation in rock 'n' roll is a hard-won battle. The dangers of mixing business and pleasure are well known in any industry, but in rock, where women are often in the minority, it is particularly important that you value your reputation. Musicians are not interested in the complications of a relationship on the road, which is why groupies were invented. Ah, the groupie, that little-understood phenomenon; the group of women, and occasionally men, that will happily sell their own mothers for a chance to do whatever it takes to get up close and personal with anyone connected with a tour. Obviously first prize for a groupie is getting with the headline artist, but hey, the management or road crew are also highly acceptable. To share in the hedonism for one night is worth any kiss-off they may receive the next day. Many truly believe that they will become the next Mrs Rock Star, but in reality most are unceremoniously sent away with nothing but memories.

From uber-cool rock tracks to heart-throb pop, my session work required me to cover many different styles of music. For producer supremo Steve Anderson I sang vocals on a track he was producing for Take That, the darlings of the teen pop scene, who were recording tracks for a new album at Sarm Studios. Steve and I had fun arranging a vocal intro on a high-energy dance track. He also booked me to sing on tracks for Kylie Minogue. Providing male vocals was Terry Ronald: singer, vocal arranger, author and all round fabulously talented guy. Terry always brought his keen sense of humour to a session; acerbic and wildly camp, he and I sang and laughed our way through the job. Both Steve and Terry have a long association with Kylie Minogue that continues to this day. The three of us were able to have even more fun together when we performed with the diminutive Miss M at Glasgow's T in the Park festival. Kylie is a delight to work with and exceptionally sweet. An absolute professional, she has sustained a very healthy career over decades.

Though in general I worked with more male than female artists, I loved working with women, and none epitomised for me the ultimate in girl-power more than Annie Lennox. I met Annie when she was asked to perform a solo show in New York's Central

Park. The band rehearsed in England and then performed a couple of gigs in Europe before flying to New York. Annie, famous for her unconventional costume choices, had Katie Kissoon and I dress as angels, complete with wings. We performed her classic hit *Walking on Broken Glass* on *The David Letterman Show*. Annie is a keenly intelligent yet grounded person and extremely easy to work with. We talked extensively about family life and the challenges of being a female on the road. She was suffering from extreme nerves at the prospect of the upcoming concert in Central Park, but successfully conquered her fears and went on to give a brilliant and memorable performance.

By now my darling friend Pepi was enjoying success as a vocal coach. People loved her approach to teaching and her philosophy that given the right instruction anyone could learn to sing. She was able to unlock vocal potential in people who would never have thought it possible. One afternoon I received a call from her.

'Darling girl,' she said, 'I'm working with a group at the moment, a bunch of young girls. They're as rough as old boots but they've got something about them.'

'OK,' I said, 'tell me more.'

'They have energy like you can't believe and the redhead's got chutzpah. They're looking for material. Have you got any songs you could send me that might suit them?'

'Well, do you think they're any good?' I replied sceptically.

'Honey, at this point I really don't know; they're not great singers,' Pepi replied. 'Plus they need another girl cos one's dropped out. So I just don't know.'

It didn't sound at all good to me, dodgy young singers looking for material and another member? Pepi found another member for them, a young girl by the name of Emma Bunton. I decided not to send them any of my songs. It was a serious error of judgment, as The Spice Girls went on to become the biggest popular cultural icons of the 1990s and a phenomenon that was to define a decade.

CHAPTER SEVEN

Baby Love

Eduardo and I had a ball living in Great Missenden, but in time we both missed the energy of the city and decided to move back to London. We found a perfect double-fronted Victorian house in Ealing. Kris and Alessia were about to move from New York to London with their mother, and Eduardo was thrilled at the idea of a settled existence for both families without the need to commute to the States every six weeks. By now I had learned more about step-parenting and I was even beginning to contemplate the idea of having children of my own.

While living in the country I was introduced to writer and television producer Nadya Sawney. Nadya approached me with her idea for a music-related TV series to be called *In an English Country Rock Garden*. The programme would document the lives and passions of rock 'n' roll stars. For generations the British aristocracy and landed gentry had owned homes with magnificent gardens and grounds, but the upkeep of these estates was astronomical, and after the social changes that followed two world wars many had been sold off. Rock stars with accumulated wealth often yearned for a country lifestyle, the perfect antidote to life on the road, and space in which to indulge their hobbies and interests. George Harrison had restored his beloved gothic pile, Friary Park in Oxfordshire, to its former glory, complete with stunning gardens. Elton John shared George's passion and did the same at his estate in Windsor. Other artists enjoyed pursuits such as owning horses and collecting classic cars. With her television background, Nadya planned to produce the series with me as executive producer and presenter. We formed a production company and produced a pilot show featuring Kenny Jones, the ex-Small Faces member and former drummer of The Who. Kenny lived at Hurtwood Park, a large estate at the foot of the Surrey Hills; besides music his passion was playing polo, and he was in the process of developing a polo club at Hurtwood. Nadya

Stewart Copeland interviewed by Tessa for In an English Country Rock Garden, with producer Nadya Sawney, Hurtwood Park Polo Club, 1994.

and I filmed a pilot for the show there and Nadya took it to the BBC, who seriously considered commissioning the series, but backed out at the 11th hour. Nadya and I were gutted. We had both believed wholeheartedly in the project and worked hard on it. It hurt to think we'd been so close to securing a deal. The disappointment stung like hell; but hey, at the end of the day that's show business for you. There are no guarantees and no one ever said it would be easy to put something like this together. The entertainment industry tested our resilience to the limit.

In 1996, shortly after the disappointment of the programme, I was recommended to record producer Pip Williams, who was working on tracks for an unbelievable achievement: a 22nd studio album for Status Quo with cover versions and guest appearances by The Beach Boys, Brian May et moi. I shared lead vocals with Francis Rossi on *Safety Dance* and with guitarist Rick Parfitt on *The Future's So Bright I Gotta Wear Shades*. For the album's promotional video, filmed in front of hundreds of loyal Quo fans, I did indeed wear shades – and a slinky little snakeskin suit. In their 39-year history it is estimated that Status Quo band members have travelled four million miles and spent a staggering 23 years away from home.

Trevor Horn's contribution to popular music has earned him the accolade 'The Man Who Invented the Eighties'. Trevor began his career as a session player and is known for a particular sensibility when working with studio musicians. From his early chart success with The Buggles and their hit single *Video Killed the Radio Star*, to his work with Frankie Goes to Hollywood, Yes and Seal, Trevor has produced countless commercially successful albums. When working with him on a session he would outline what was needed on a particular track, but never over-instructed. Trevor hired people for their ideas and interpretation and, although never articulated, he clearly expected to be impressed. If he was, this otherwise quiet northerner came alive. Sometimes he would ask me to sing exactly like the lead singer, and then skilfully marry my vocal with the artist's. No one would be aware that an additional voice was there, it simply added colour or texture to the track. When Trevor heard an idea that inspired him he would allow you to follow the creative path and expand upon it. Consequently, I always wanted to please him more than any other producer and believe I have done my best work with him.

On Tina Turner's *Wildest Dreams* album I had the opportunity to work with my good friend Miriam Stockley. Blessed with rare skill, Miriam is the perfect session singer and has one of the most beautiful voices I have ever heard. An extraordinary technician, she also has her own sound: an instantly recognisable solo voice. I adored working with Miri, and working with her and Trevor was a dream come true. Tina applied her signature powerhouse vocals to each track on *Wildest Dreams*, including the James Bond theme for *GoldenEye* and duets with Barry White, Sting and Antonio Banderas. In the UK, the album went double platinum.

Later that year the Eric Clapton band performed a concert in Hyde Park, London that was filmed for release on DVD. The band line-up had undergone changes with the addition of session drummer Steve Gadd, bass player Dave Bronze, Chris Stainton on keyboards, Jerry Portnoy on harmonica and a brass section. In addition, Roddy Lorimer, Simon Clarke and Tim Sanders lent a different feel to Eric's songs. From the *August* album, *Holy Mother* was included in the set with soulful vocals from Katie and The

East London Gospel Choir. The show was hugely successful and Eric, looking relaxed in leather jacket and jeans, seemed happier than I'd seen him in a while.

In 1997 Eduardo and I had been together for eight years and I'd gone from having no experience with children to being an integral part of Kris and Alessia's lives. A chance conversation with my mother that summer had given me food for thought. Molly had never put pressure on me to have children and had never questioned my decision to prioritise my career, but over afternoon tea one day she turned to me and said, 'Be careful not to wait too long to have children my darling, I'd hate for you to miss out on the opportunity.' Without agenda, her remark simply stated her desire for me to experience having children of my own. Perhaps she saw that at 35 my window of opportunity was closing. My mother had watched me gain confidence as I grew into my role as a step-parent and I'm sure she also knew that it was important for Eduardo and me to take the next step.

Molly's wise words resonated that day and stayed with me. I began to realise it was time to make some decisions; my work schedule was not as frantic as it had been and Eric was not touring as much as before, so I decided to stop taking the contraceptive pill. I knew that the effects of taking the pill could take a while to leave my system and thought this would probably take about a year. On 7 June I organised a go-karting party for Eduardo's 40th birthday. A small group of friends spent the afternoon haring around the indoor track and celebrated afterwards with champagne and cake. That night I conceived, and a few weeks later when I discovered I was pregnant, was unsure as to what Eduardo's reaction would be. We had discussed having children many times, but he was still involved in an acrimonious relationship with Paola, his not-yet-ex-wife and seemed to be coping with constant strain. When I shared the news, Eduardo was surprised and at first I interpreted this as disappointment. He knew full well the weight of responsibility that parenthood brings, and for a couple of days his concerns outweighed the joy. As time went on though, the concerns faded with the realisation that we were going to have a child of our own. The chance to work with Joe Cocker on his *Across From Midnight* album came as a welcome distraction from the business of acute morning sickness.

'Are there twins in the family?' asked the nurse casually as she rolled the ultrasound ball over my expanding tummy.

She had our full attention as Eduardo and I stared wide-eyed at the monitor in front of us.

'Now, can you see what I'm seeing on the screen? If I move the ultrasound over this way we can see a baby,' she said, moving the probe. 'And if I move it over here...'

I understood in an instant what the nurse was saying.

'Sweetheart, are you OK? Can you believe it? Oh my God... we're having twins.'

Eduardo's face was a picture, his mouth open in disbelief.

'Seriously though, how could it not have occurred to me that I might have twins when my father was one?' I asked.

'You're right to think that,' said the nurse. 'Your babies are in fact fraternal twins and that's hereditary: the result of two individual eggs being fertilised. Congratulations to you both.'

We were swiftly moving from having two children to four. The revelation came as a huge surprise to both of us, but surprise turned to joy as we realised how fortunate we were. Standing outside the Harley Street clinic, Eduardo and I shared our news by phone with the family, who were absolutely thrilled. For Molly, it had special meaning; she loved the idea of continuing the Webb tradition of twins. Kris and Alessia were excited at the prospect of two brothers or two sisters, or perhaps one of each.

When I thought about it, I was relieved that Eduardo and I were on the road to having a family of our own; after so many years together we needed to cement our relationship and joked that the afternoon of karting on Eduardo's birthday must have contributed to me producing two eggs: a clear case of never an egg around when you want one, and then two at once!

The doctors had pronounced me fit and healthy enough to travel, so I embarked on the Eric Clapton band annual tour of Japan. At the beginning of the pregnancy I had experienced some health issues, but at six months I was now feeling great. This would be my only tour while pregnant, as it would not be advisable to fly thereafter. Kitting myself out with some swanky maternity clothes, I embarked on the 11½-hour flight to Tokyo.

People treat you with a certain reverence when you're pregnant; the band became ultra-protective of me, and Eric was warm and supportive. I felt really well and had no problems after the long flight from London other than the usual extreme jet lag. As always, Katie was amazing and shared her own pregnancy stories with me. She and I ran through endless name ideas and I could not have asked for the company of a more loving friend. Eric has always had a special connection with Japanese audiences, who are more attuned to listening than anywhere else in the world. When I first began working there the crowds clapped quietly and respectfully after every song, there was no whooping or cheering, but over the years the audiences had changed and become more animated. Always a lover of Japanese cuisine, I've eaten some of the finest there. Eric would often invite Katie and me to have supper with him and one evening he took us to a place he called 'the shouting restaurant'. This fish restaurant in downtown Tokyo had a tradition of waiters shouting their orders from one side of the room to the other. The place was bustling and very noisy, but so much fun as dish upon dish of exquisite food was served.

In the battle to conquer his addiction to alcohol, Eric had for years been committed to the Alcoholics Anonymous programme and would attend meetings wherever we were in the world. During the day he'd quietly show up at a meeting unannounced to listen and share whatever he needed to. I often imagined the surprise of other members when Eric Clapton arrived out of the blue. AA provided the support network Eric needed, and he was doing really well. At the end of every tour the band were treated to a day at a traditional Japanese bath house by the promoter of the shows, Mr Udo. At the bathhouse, wearing only a large pair of paper panties, you were scrubbed down vigorously by a robust Japanese woman. You were then bathed and finally massaged, breasts and all, to within an inch of your life by another small but deceptively powerful woman. Just when you thought you must be missing several layers of skin from all the scrubbing and rubbing, you were served a rejuvenating bowl of Japanese noodles. Though normally happy to indulge in the bathing ritual, while pregnant I thought it better to abstain for fear of bringing on an early labour.

Christmas that year was celebrated with the family at our house. Molly, Amanda, Ian, Janet, Kris and Alessia and Eduardo's young niece Jana and nephew Eddie spent the holidays with us. The house was packed to the gills with children and animals, just the way we liked it. Despite my girth increasing by the day I relished the preparations for Christmas and the imminent arrival of the twins.

On the morning of 10 February 1998 I posed for last-minute photos outside the house before we left for the Queen Charlotte hospital. Having opted for an elected Caesarian section, I knew the date the babies would arrive. Shortly after one in the afternoon I gave birth to twin daughters, Mikaela Frances and Fallon Alexandra, and, with what seemed like crowds of healthcare professionals in the operating theatre, there were no complications. Back in my hospital room, woozy and exhausted, I was surrounded by family and close friends oohing and aahing over our two noticeably different-looking babies. With Eduardo's mixed-race background, we'd thought the gene pool might produce an interesting combination in our twins, but neither of us was prepared for the startling differences between them; Mikaela was fair-haired, light-skinned and blue-eyed, Fallon was dark-haired and darker skinned with brown eyes. Both had heads of thick hair and both were the most beautiful babies I had ever seen. The bond was instant, but so was the sense of responsibility and the awareness that when Eduardo and I left the security of the hospital we would be on our own. Had Molly been younger she would have willingly helped us with the early challenges, but she was not entirely well. Eduardo and I arrived home with our two bundles and set up camp in the living room so I did not constantly have to go up and down stairs.

Every parent knows how overwhelming a new baby is, so two were a challenge. Eduardo was caring and fully hands-on, his previous experience coming to the fore. Patient and supportive, he was deeply in love with his new daughters. It was chaotic in the early weeks as we grabbed cold food and sleep between feeding, bathing and caring for two demanding babies. At the beginning of the second month Eduardo announced that he would have to travel to Mozambique for two weeks. Nervous at the idea of me being alone, we looked into employing a maternity nurse for the time that Eduardo would be away and finally settled on an Irish ex-nun, with over 20 years' experience of newborns. With Eduardo gone, Nurse Alison arrived at the house in her crisply starched uniform with upside-down watch pinned to the top pocket. From the start she meant business. Looking around the dishevelled house, she picked up half-finished bottles of milk with barely contained disapproval.

'Well now, we'll need to get their feeding sorted first,' she sniffed in her broad Irish accent. Like Mary Poppins, I half-expected her to pull her belongings out of a carpet bag and shout 'spit spot.'

'We'll also get their sleeping routine organised as soon as we can,' she said, checking her watch.

'What about you?' I offered. 'I've set up a bed for you upstairs and...'

'Oh don't worry about me, dear, I don't need to sleep. You just worry about yourself. Now, shall we have some tea?'

A direct, no-nonsense woman, Alison immediately organised the babies and me into a firm routine. She worked 24 hours a day, grabbing cat-naps when she could. Her presence was hugely reassuring and I was happy to follow the newly implemented rules. With so many options available to a new mother it's great to have

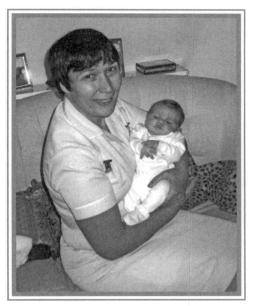

Alison the maternity nurse working her magic with Mikaela, Ealing, 1998.

someone who's familiar with tried and tested methods. Alison knew her stuff.

'Ah to be sure there's no such thing as colic,' she announced one morning when we were busy winding the princesses.

'What do you mean? There's medicine for it and all the books talk about it,' I replied.

'It's basically trapped air and you've just got to get it out. Even if we have to sit here bouncing babies till St Patrick's Day, we'll get that wind up.'

Alison knew everything and was old-school in every way. For her, routine was the key to a contented baby and happy parents. She would have none of the new-fangled theories of holding your baby ad nauseam or of them sleeping in the parental bed. Her traditional methods were not for the faint-hearted and from day one she advocated leaving the twins to cry 'till they'd got it out of their system'.

Though extraordinarily difficult, this worked, and Nurse Alison swiftly got my two babes into a sleep pattern that for some parents would have been a step too far, but made absolute sense to me. Feeding was timed to the minute, and if you were late Alison had no difficulty voicing her disapproval. Once she gave me the death stare for serving her a less than piping hot cup of tea, but as I said, she was from the old school. I was relieved that Eduardo was away as I don't think he would have been able to endure the implementation of 'the rules' and the nights of leaving our babies to 'cry it out'. But every day with Alison brought about a growing sense of confidence in me; the system she established worked for the twins and me, but might not have worked for everyone. When Eduardo returned from his business trip he found two happy and contented babies, a calm and tidy house and a wife who was not stressed out of her coconut from sleep deprivation. After she departed, we stuck to Alison's routine for the better part of two years.

Molly Webb with her twin granddaughters, Ealing, 1998.

When Mikaela and Fallon were four months old I was booked to work on a large choir session for Sarah Brightman. *Eden* was to be her sixth solo album. I hadn't seen Sarah since being married to Richard. She'd come a long way since then and had built a highly successful career as a classical crossover soprano. On the day of the session I had arranged with Eduardo that he would return home at four o'clock to take over looking after the twins. Katie and I would then drive together to the session at Angel Studios. Katie arrived at the house at four and we waited for Eduardo to return. It was getting late. I tried to stay calm as I dialled Eduardo.

'Honey, where are you?' I asked hastily. 'Are you nearly at the house?'

Eduardo explained that he was stuck in traffic.

'Are you kidding me? You said you'd be back in time to look after the girls. Katie and I have to leave now, the traffic's going to be a nightmare. Yes, yes I know, but we have no choice, we'll just have to take them with us. Listen, gotta go, bye.'

'Come on Tess, we can do this. We'll meet Eduardo on the road,' laughed Katie as she sprang into action, scooping up a baby and dashing towards the front door. 'Have you got nappies and food?'

'How can you think about eating at a time like this?' I joked. Oh my God, I'm gonna kill him when I see him.

Katie and I bundled the girls into their car seats and set off at a furious pace for the studio. We were now running late and the traffic was really bad as we drove across town to the north of London. The longer we sat in the traffic, the more stressed I became, and in spite of Katie's calming words we both knew we could not afford to have the rest of the choir wait for us. Sensing my tension, the louder Miki and Fallon wailed.

'Try singing to them, Katie, they love music. Do you know *The Itsy Bitsy Spider?*'

Katie gave me a withering look. 'Hah, do I know *The Itsy Bitsy Spider?* I practically wrote it.'

Despite having the children's classic sung in harmony by two seasoned professionals, nothing would soothe them. By the time we reached the studio I was rigid with tension; we were late for the session and I had no plan about what to do with the babies. The assembled choir turned to watch as we barged in, each clutching a very unhappy twin. What the hell was I going to do now?

'Hi everyone. I'm so incredibly sorry to keep you all waiting,' I said while scanning the studio for anyone I could leave the babies with. Then suddenly I had an idea.

'Just give me one second, literally one second.'

A drum booth is a small soundproof room designed to house the drum kit in a studio; its purpose is to isolate sound and prevent unwanted vibrations from the drums leaking on to other microphones. Perfect! Grabbing both the girls, who were still howling, I placed them on the floor of the drum booth and shut the soundproof sliding doors. Pausing for a second, I breathed a sigh of relief as my plan seemed to work and began to routine the song with Katie and the rest of the choir. When Sarah Brightman came out of the control room and said hello to everyone, she hugged me warmly and we commented on how long it had been since we'd seen each other. We began to record, and for the first time since leaping out of the car I started to relax. But the choir only got as far as the first few lines when the twins started up again – this time with a vengeance – we could hear them through the soundproof doors. I now had no alternative but to excuse myself from the session and remove the wailers. To my surprise, Sarah and the sound engineer came through into the recording room and slid open the drum booth doors. Without saying a word, each picked up an infant, walked back into the control room, sat down and proceeded to bounce a baby on their knee, achieving almost instantaneous quiet. I wish I'd been able to capture the image of the two of them conducting the session, each jiggling a bemused infant. How Sarah Brightman, the superstar soprano, who has no children of her own, knew that this would be the solution I will never know. She and the engineer coped beautifully until Eduardo arrived to relieve them of their duties. The job was finished on time and everyone was thrilled with the results, but I shall never forget how Sarah's kindness and quick thinking got me through the most nerve-wracking recording session of my life.

The artist Ronan Keating had fought his way through the trials and tribulations of being in a boy band, and was building a solo career for himself. Miriam Stockley and I were asked to sing on tracks for Ronan by producer Steve Lipson, whom I had worked with regularly over the years. Working with Miri was a treat and would always inspire me to raise my game. Steve had strong ideas about what he wanted on the songs but allowed Miri and me the latitude to construct our vocal parts. On one track, a lilting country song, we layered thick harmonies to create a lush sound behind Ronan's plaintive lead vocal. *When You Say Nothing At All* was released as part of the soundtrack for the blockbuster film *Notting Hill*. It was Ronan's debut solo single and shot to number one in the UK, Ireland and New Zealand.

The singing voice of a good back-up singer has to be as flexible as an actor's with the spoken word. The ability to sing in any style and to be able to move between different genres is crucial. Studio work and live work require different skills. When working on stage it's all about the performance, which means looking amazing, and generally as sexy as possible, and making the artist feel you are about him or her: that your vocals complement them 100 per cent. In the studio, the requirement is to be able to evaluate every job quickly and with little or no instruction; a studio singer has to be able to work out the harmonies and create an entire vocal arrangement for the track. Whether singing behind the artist in the studio or working alongside them in a live situation, you need to know who you are and what to do. According to Lisa Fischer, who sings with The Rolling Stones, 'I reject the notion that the job you excel at is somehow not enough to aspire to, that there has to be something more. I love supporting other artists.'

My babies were growing up, and after a year of what seemed endless bottles, nappy changes and full-on attention, life became easier. With the help of a young nanny, Tizzie Hall, I was now firmly into the swing of motherhood. Tizzie, with her boundless energy and confidence, was a huge help. Eduardo was back at work and I was able to take on more jobs again. Tizzie has since gone on to become a leading authority on babies, and has published numerous books as 'The Baby Whisperer'.

Aged 13, Kristofer was about to move to a new school in Highgate. Eduardo and I felt it made sense for us to live nearby

Eduardo and Tessa, 2001.

and were also thinking ahead to when Mikaela and Fallon would begin their schooling. I'd always liked an area called Hadley Wood in Hertfordshire, a little piece of heaven with its attractive houses, good schools, and proximity to London.

This rock chick was about to give suburbia the seal of approval.

CHAPTER EIGHT

At the Court of King Robbie

Hook End Manor studios in the heart of the Oxfordshire countryside were once owned by Dave Gilmour of Pink Floyd. The residential studio was then taken over by Trevor Horn. Guy Chambers, the keyboard player I'd first met on the Jimmy Nail tour, asked me to work on an album at Hook End that he was producing for pop sensation Robbie Williams. Robbie first achieved fame with the phenomenally successful Take That, and after going solo formed a partnership with Guy Chambers that resulted in hits such as *Angels, Let Me Entertain You* and *Millennium.* With Guy producing, Robbie was fast becoming an unstoppable force in British pop music.

Arriving at the studio for the day's vocals with my trusty cohorts, Katie Kissoon and Sylvia Mason, we were introduced to Robbie, who hugged us warmly. Much taller than we'd imagined, he was breathtakingly handsome with green eyes and an engaging grin. Then and there I knew we were done for; the girls and I were officially under the RW spell to which countless other females had fallen victim, and were now his vocal slaves.

Guy Chambers played us the first track, an unapologetic disco anthem complete with pumping bass line and the opening words:

'Me with the floorshow, kicking with your torso,

Boys getting high and the girls even more so.

Wave your hands if you're not with a man,

Can I kick it?'

To which Katie, Sylvia and I dutifully responded, 'Yes you can!' *Rock DJ* was to become a party track of note with its call and answer vocals. It was clear to all of us that it would be a smash hit, and we had enormous fun recording it with Robbie, who joined in with us on the choruses. For the same album Katie, Sylvia and I recorded vocals on *Kids*, a duet with Robbie and Australian pop icon Kylie Minogue. *Rock DJ* quickly rose to number one in the UK charts and was played literally everywhere. The album, *Sing While You're Winning*, became the bestselling album of 2000.

Katie Kissoon, Tessa and Robbie Williams recording vocals for Rock DJ in the studio at Hook End, 2000.

After we'd made several TV appearances with him, Robbie asked if Katie and I would join his touring band. I hesitated, as the twins were 18 months old and touring was not really what I had in mind now I had children. Work with Eric Clapton had slowed and I felt my touring days were pretty much behind me. The practicalities of being away from the family for six weeks at a time would not be easy to organise and I still harboured fears about how spending time apart could impact on my relationship – a hangover from my days with The Police. Financially, however, touring was tempting, so Eduardo and I discussed the proposal at length and eventually decided that if we hired a really good nanny and were not apart for more than three weeks at a stretch, we could make it work.

And so it came about: Ms Niles was hitting the road again!

Rehearsals for Robbie Williams' Sermon on the Mount tour began in a decidedly un-rock 'n' roll location near Bath in Somerset, where Robbie had rented a Grade I listed manor house nestled in a secluded valley in which to live and rehearse. St Catherine's Court, we learned, was built by one John Cantlow, a prior of Bath Abbey in the 1480s.

In 1984 the estate was bought by actress Jane Seymour, who spent millions on its refurbishment. She and her film producer husband decided to rent the house out as a film set and recording studio. Robbie felt the genteel setting was the perfect place to rehearse for his tour, so the band, equipment and entourage moved in. Each band member chose a bedroom, with Robbie in The Seymour Suite. With a housekeeper, chef and staff, we were

Rehearsing for the Robbie Williams tour 2001,
(L to R) Tessa, Claire Worrall and Katie Kissoon.

cocooned in our own private world, away from the prying eyes of the media. The long summer days of 2000 were filled with music and a great deal of laughter. After a hearty breakfast each morning, the band would rehearse in the Great Hall under the guidance and watchful eye of Guy Chambers, our commander-in-chief.

Just before rehearsals began, Eduardo and I went about finding a nanny for Mikaela and Fallon. Agencies sent us suitable candidates whom we began interviewing. We needed a balance: someone with experience and credentials but who could be flexible with their time, as I would be working unusual hours. The candidate also had to be loving and fun. After several unsuitable applicants we began to feel disheartened. One girl we saw arrived at the house a nervous wreck. Now I know interviews can be daunting, but this young lady was sweating and falling over her words from the moment she arrived. I tried my best to put her at ease, but when she noticed that Fallon was sucking her thumb she exclaimed, 'Oh, I see they're sum fuckers – oh shit – sorry, I mean they're thumb suckers.' I thought the poor girl was going to expire, she was so embarrassed. Shame, I felt sorry for her but no, she didn't get the job.

Thirty-one-year-old Emily Karagozlou walked through the front door with an air of confidence and self-assurance about her. You know how you get a vibe about someone immediately? Well, I did with Emily. Her interview went really well; she was relaxed, professional and had everything that Eduardo and I were looking for in a nanny. Her references were exemplary, she was unfazed by the unusual working hours and she seemed a fun person. Mikaela, Fallon and Emily took to each other immediately, and she became their nanny without further ado. It was a huge relief for Eduardo and me to know that our precious girls were in safe hands; it allowed us to work without anxiety and, as a bonus, Emily's favourite artist was none other than my current boss.

Ensconced at St Catherine's Court, Robbie Williams and the 15-piece band worked hard and were soon sounding great. The rhythm section comprised the diminutive Scouser Chris Sharrock on drums, Yolanda Charles, an accomplished bassist whose great sound and willowy good looks were easy on the senses, and guitar player/vocalist, Gary Nuttall. Then there was Claire Worrall, whose keyboard musicianship and attractive personality were the band's secret weapons. Mild-mannered Melvyn Duffy was a magnificent pedal steel guitar player and, on guitar and vocals, Fil Eisler, another superb musician and hit with the ladies, was a keen wearer of the kilt. Alongside Katie and myself was our musical director, Guy Chambers. The brass section included a crack British team: Steve Sidwell, Chris White, Paul Spong, Simon Gardener, Neil Sidwell and Dave Bishop.

Over six weeks the band became a family. Cut off from the outside world and living and working together 24/7, we got to know each other well. After long days of rehearsals we dined at the Court of King Robbie in the manor's orangery and spent the evenings relaxing in the library or playing games around a roaring fire. Robbie liked all kinds of games.

One morning Robbie appeared at the breakfast table looking devilishly handsome but somewhat perplexed. Running his hand through his dishevelled hair he said quietly, 'I'm a bit confused, something weird just happened.'

Checking to make sure the housekeeper, who was preparing breakfast, couldn't hear, Robbie sat down.

'Yeah, so it's like this, right. I'm lying in bed half asleep when I hear this noise and I realise that someone's come into the room.'

'What, they didn't knock or leave when they saw you were in bed?' I asked.

'Well that was what was so weird,' said Robbie, drawing hard on his cigarette.

'It was the cleaner and she just starts dusting the furniture around me. So I pulled up the duvet and let her get on with it.'

'Next thing I know, she's only gone and pulled back the covers and starts doin' the business.'

The table erupted with laughter as Robbie whispered, 'Listen, I know the staff are under instructions to accommodate me but that's taking it a bit far even for me.'

'God yes, she could have been a complete weirdo or anything,' piped in Chris Sharrock.

Though hilarious, we all agreed that it could have been dangerous.

Robbie had no desire to get the perpetrator into trouble, but upon investigation the story revealed was unexpected. St Catherine's Court was situated in a tiny hamlet, and with little or no crime in the area, the house doors were rarely locked during the day. It would appear that on hearing Robbie was staying there a young girl from a neighbouring village seized the opportunity to come by and take a look around. Unseen by the staff, she'd snuck in through the back door, found her way through the kitchens, up the back staircase and into Robbie's bedroom. Her ingenious plan had worked like a dream. In the cold light of day, of course, the intruder's breach of security was cause for concern and had to be taken seriously, as her intentions could have been sinister; over the years Robbie had had to deal with his fair share of stalkers and opportunists. On this occasion, however, no charges were laid and the perpetrator became affectionately referred to by the band as 'Morning Glory'.

In October 2000 the Sermon on the Mount Tour commenced in Reading, a deliberately low-key gig so that any last-minute crinkles could be ironed out before the tour hit the bigger cities. The Birmingham, Glasgow, Newcastle, Manchester and London concerts were incredible; the band's sound was tight and Robbie lit up on stage, his boundless energy powering through old and new favourites. Being on stage with him was a whole new kind of fun for me. Performing with Eric had always been fantastic, his music and musicians being undeniably among the best in the world, but at 26 years old Robbie was a brilliant showman who ignited the band every night, which encouraged everyone to constantly better their own performances in an attempt to equal his — a combined energy that made each show electrifying. Robbie set the tone and the musicians were happy to follow his lead. Surprisingly, Rob would come off stage some nights and complain that he had not had a good show or that he felt his performance had been off. In my opinion he was never less than at his best.

Robbie was a fantastic boss and generous in his praise to others. Contrary to what many people saw as his arrogant, nonchalant on-stage persona, he was a focused and inspiring leader. I remember having a conversation with him about his success. At the time, Robbie was at the zenith of his career

'You know what,' he said, 'this is my time right now but the public are fickle and I might be out of fashion in a few years, you just never know.'

I remember being impressed that he could articulate the pitfalls of show business. For a young man at the height of his success he understood clearly that fame can be transitory. For someone immersed in success, Robbie's objectivity indicated high intelligence and maturity beyond his years. His charm was infectious and he had a keen sense of mischief, but come show-time he was entirely professional.

Before each show Robbie and the singers gathered in the band room for the obligatory vocal warm-up, then came the rituals of pre-show preparation. The dressing area, often a cavernous locker room, provided great acoustics for practising scales and harmonies. In the girls' dressing room the theatre-style lights around the mirrors dazzled, and clouds of hairspray and glitter floated down like rain. In the next room the drummer practised intricate paradiddles on the arm of a leather sofa, the guitar player called out to the frazzled wardrobe mistress for his favourite kilt and the bass player relayed careful instructions to her roadie. A clatter on the door signalled five minutes before show-time. Words of encouragement were exchanged in a final scramble for shoes, cigarettes, vodka and cups of honey and lemon tea. Monitors were secured to clothing by nimble-fingered minions and voices harmonised, flexible and fluid from their warm-ups. Outside the dressing rooms the corridors bustled with security guards, managers and assistants eager to escort the anointed ones to the altar. The atmosphere intensified as the stadium buzzed with anticipation and the house lights were lowered. Two-way radios hissed instructions as the band neared the stage and paused at the steps to link arms with one another and bow their heads as Robbie conducted the prayer.

Robbie: Elvis, grant me the serenity to accept the things I cannot change

Band: Uh huh

Robbie: The courage to change the things I can

Band: Uh huh

Robbie: And the wisdom to know the difference

Band: Thank you very much

In 2001 Robbie and the band returned to the studio to record a track titled *Not of This Earth* written for the film *Bridget Jones's Diary*. Robbie's new Weddings, Bar Mitzvahs and Stadiums Tour then rolled out across Europe and South East Asia. For the

Australian and New Zealand dates the tour was renamed Sing When You're Pacific Rimming. Musical director Guy Chambers ran a tight ship and the band were slick and polished. During a short break in the tour schedule, guitar player Gary Nuttall and I went into the studio to sing guide vocals on a track called *Somethin' Stupid*. The song originally made famous by Frank and Nancy Sinatra was then reworked by Robbie and Academy Award winning actress, Nicole Kidman. Nicole used my singing as a guide when it came to recording her vocals. Released in November, *Somethin' Stupid* became Robbie's first Christmas number one.

So far, I'd been privy to the benefits and the perils of stardom, the lack of privacy and the constant intrusions in an artist's life. The public's expectation that you are a performer both on and off stage is, at best, unrealistic. Certainly the financial rewards are there, but at what price to your sanity? It's almost impossible to stay grounded when you are treated differently because of your star status. The partner of a celebrity is often long suffering and has to deal with fidelity issues as well as an entire entourage of people who are paid to indulge their loved one's every need. In a touring situation the temptations for the artist are immense. Throw drugs and alcohol into the pot, and you have a really complicated and potentially destructive situation.

In Manchester the band performed for three nights at the historic Old Trafford ground, so Eduardo and the twins and nanny, Emily, were able to visit. It was fantastic having them come as I was finding it tough being away from the family. Concerns about spending too long away from home still haunted me and even though Emily provided the best care for my girls and loved them as her own, I felt torn. I really hadn't had children to then go back on the road. It wasn't part of my plan. But then, when does life ever go as planned? The tour was a sell-out, Robbie was a massively successful recording artist and the band was paid handsomely. It was a dream gig, a great boss and fabulous co-workers, but back in my hotel room after the shows I felt a powerful sense of sadness and missed Eduardo and the kids more than I wanted to admit. Eduardo's work dictated that he too needed to travel. Could we continue to sustain a relationship with both of us travelling, and was it the best thing for our children? These were questions that would continue to trouble me in the months ahead.

The last dates of Robbie's tour came to a close in New Zealand and I flew the 15½ hours to South Africa for a much-needed family holiday. While there, I received the sad news that George Harrison had died. George had suffered from lung cancer for some time, but the news still came as a shock. He was only 58 years old. I treasured the memories of George, who had always shown me such kindness and generosity. For my father's funeral he and Olivia had sent the most beautiful flowers, and the memory of George's wry humour and friendship on the tour of Japan will never fade. Then there were the fabulous parties he hosted at Friary Park and his thoughtful gifts over the years, my favourite being a small leather-bound book containing some of his sage lyrics. Most of all there was his music. For me, being able to share in making music with George was the greatest gift of all. After the Japanese tour, he had commissioned a limited edition book. Each member of the band wrote their own chapter, recalling personal memories of the tour. In my copy George wrote: 'To Tessa, with love & thanks for the lovely memory, GH. PS I think your chapter is the best!' Ever the joker, I wouldn't be surprised if George had written the same dedication to every musician. In George's own chapter he wrote: 'Musicians have always been, in a way, special to me. Music is a living thing and it's created from a force within. I like anything as long as it's good and made by people not machines.' I have never worked with a musician who respected his fellow musicians as much as George Harrison. In my own chapter I recalled the night that George came off stage after a blisteringly good performance and said to me, 'I don't know about this performing lark, I don't know whether I'm cut out for it.'

Family life and session work continued to keep me busy with jobs for ex-Spice Girl Geri Halliwell, Natalie Imbruglia and voiceovers for TV commercials. My mother, Molly, had been ill for some time and was taken into hospital. The previous year she had been diagnosed with skin cancer and had taken the news of her diagnosis with extraordinary grace. She had not been truly well for years but had stoically carried on, often neglecting her health needs. The doctors now informed her that the disease was terminal, but that they could offer her the usual bouts of chemo and radiotherapy. Molly declined, saying she would rather live out the time she had left without subjecting herself to the ravages of treatment. Initially it was hard for Amanda, Ian and me to accept her decision as treatment might have prolonged her life, but ultimately we respected her wishes.

Molly was living in an apartment she had inherited from her brother Tony, and continued throughout her illness to live by herself, staunchly guarding her independence. As she saw it, she did not want to be a burden to her children. It was desperately hard for us to see our mother growing weaker as she attempted to hide her discomfort. She was of the pre-World War II 'Buckle down and get on with it' generation and underplayed her needs most of the time. When war broke out Molly was one of the youngest volunteers to sign up for army duty, and truth be told, perhaps to get away from her domineering father. My grandfather Percy, a post office employee at the outbreak of war, was recruited to work in the Cabinet War Rooms, an underground complex that housed the British Government Command Centre. According to Molly, her father had a photographic memory and could pinpoint any area on a map of Great Britain at a glance. In the months leading up to her father's deployment in Winston Churchill's map room, she recalled being regularly followed home from school by members of British Intelligence.

Molly had signed up to 'do her bit' for the war effort when still a teenager. Understandably, once the war was over many who had served in the armed forces from 1939 to 1945 felt the imperative to rebuild their families, a profound need to move forward with their lives and put the horrors of war behind them. My parents would occasionally talk about their participation during those testing times, but for the most part it remained a chapter of their lives they preferred to consign to the past.

With no touring dates confirmed with Robbie or Eric at this point, I was able to spend time with Molly. Amanda, Ian and I were acutely aware that time with our mother was precious. Mikaela and Fallon were due to start 'big school' in September 2002 and Molly so wanted to see her granddaughters in their school uniform. Ian and partner Christien had a beautiful two-year-old daughter named Stella, and as a family we tried to make the most of the time Molly had left.

Eduardo and I decided that as the twins were about to start school we could no longer justify employing a full-time nanny. It was hard to say goodbye to Emily, who had been the very best nanny we could have wished for. Without her constant and loving support that went way beyond her job description, Eduardo and I could never have achieved the things we'd set out to do.

Molly celebrated her 77th birthday surrounded by family and was able to look at photographs of the twins in their new school uniforms. She was now at a hospice, frail but still somehow managing to retain her humour and her unceasing interest in people. At any given time Molly shared a ward with two others, whom she would immediately befriend. In true Molly fashion she would enjoy to the full the brief friendships with these women who shared the same situation as her, never mind that sometimes their relationships lasted only a few days. Kindred spirits, they were there for the same reason and nearing the end of their journeys too. As her new acquaintances passed away, Molly would befriend the next two, knowing that at any time it would be her turn. I have no doubt that these relationships were meaningful to her; the imperative to connect with people, however fleetingly, was important to her and she remained lucid, courageous, empathetic and kind to the end of her life.

Shortly before her death, the entire family including Kristofer, Alessia, Mikaela, Fallon and little Stella visited Molly. Struggling with my own emotions and wishing to shield the children from the unpleasantness of her condition, I suggested that the kids should not see Grandma, but remember her the way she had been. Thirteen-year-old Alessia had always had a special relationship with Molly and possessed the maturity of someone way beyond her years. Alessia stated that she thought it would be a good thing for all the grandchildren to say their goodbyes to Molly. She was right of course, and somehow knew instinctively what needed to be done. She and Kris took Fallon, Mikaela and Stella into Molly's room where she was 'sleeping' and gently encouraged the little ones to kiss their Grandma goodbye. I shall be eternally grateful for Alessia's presence of mind that day; she knew exactly the right thing to do and quietly led the way. Molly died on Sunday 11 August 2002, leaving a hole in all our hearts.

CHAPTER NINE

Skating on thin ice

After Molly's funeral, Eduardo and I took our three girls on a good old British family holiday. Initially I had difficulty convincing my beloved that we'd have a great time even if the weather was characteristically crap. Childhood holidays had for me been simple affairs: caravanning and holiday camps, candy floss, lilos, mini-golf and donkey rides. I don't remember the weather. When you're a kid there are only two important things: either you're having fun or you're not.

My parents would always enter Amanda and me in the local fancy dress competition. One memorable year Amanda went dressed as Nell Gwynne, complete with a basket full of oranges, and I went as a rat. When I was 11, my family spent a week at a Butlins holiday camp. Eager as always to perform, I entered the talent competition and sang *Raindrops Keep Falling on My Head* and played a rendition of *Edelweiss* on the treble recorder, and won first prize. My treasured dress, from the Ladybird shop, was the first that wasn't a hand-me-down from Amanda. My hair, styled by Molly, was parted so low on the side of my head that it began just above my ear. The prize was a week's holiday to another Butlins camp in glamorous Bognor Regis, but I suffered a bitter disappointment when Molly and Len wouldn't allow me to go because of school exams.

Eduardo, on the other hand, had grown up in the tropics, swimming in warm oceans lapping against white sandy beaches. While I chased pigeons along the seafront, Eduardo watched flamingos wading in crystal clear waters. While I made a stick of rock last for two days, Eduardo ate fresh prawns. Eduardo's father had once had to rescue his son from the ocean when he became entangled in the venomous tentacles of a Portuguese man o' war. Len's only contact with the deep was lying on a towel reading a copy of *Jaws*.

Saunton Sands in Devon was the perfect holiday spot. We spent long days building sand castles on the beach and drinking Heinz tomato soup from a flask for lunch. Feeling nostalgic, I needed to reconnect with the simplicity of my much-loved childhood holidays and create some new memories with my family.

Studio work with Robbie resumed in July at Sir George Martin's Air Lyndhurst studios. Robbie was busy recording demos for a new album with Guy Chambers, and Katie and I worked on a song called *Something Beautiful*. Originally penned by Messrs Chambers and Williams for Tom Jones, it was released on Robbie's album *Escapology*. Robbie had just signed a record-breaking £8 million contract with EMI and was at the top of his game. He was also experiencing newfound confidence in his own songwriting. Three songs written by Robbie appeared on

Escapology, signalling the beginning of a breakaway from his partner of several years, Guy Chambers.

My five-year-old daughters were about to start big school. Every parent can attest to this being a huge step for children and parents alike, but the emotions I felt watching my girls walk through the gates on that first day were bittersweet. You know that this will be a defining moment for them, but will they enjoy it? School is a bigger world, and kids and parents can sometimes be mean. On that first day it was hard to keep my emotions in check. As a responsible parent I was supposed to convince the girls that going to school was a huge adventure and not at all scary. Right then, the urge to run away and join a travelling circus was profound.

In October 2002 the Robbie Williams band were busy rehearsing for his upcoming TV special. Filmed at the famous Pinewood Studios just before the release of the *Escapology* album, the show had a similar feel to Elvis Presley's 1968 Comeback Television Special. Complete with female dancers and full orchestra, the look of the show was undeniably retro. Dazzlingly handsome, Robbie's performance was faultless.

The following month I received a call from Eric Clapton. Olivia Harrison had asked Eric if he would put a band together for a memorial concert to celebrate the first anniversary of George's death. Eric asked if I would like to be part of the commemoration. The rehearsals were held over ten days at the Sanctuary Asylum Studios in London. The band – actually more of a supergroup – was made up of George's closest friends. When word got out about the rehearsals, musicians began showing up at the studios asking for a chance to play. Unfortunately they were turned away because, as it was, the band was rather large. And what a band it was:

> *Eric Clapton – Guitars and Musical Director*
>
> *Jeff Lynne, Tom Petty, Joe Brown, Albert Lee, Marc Mann, Andy Fairweather Low, Dhani Harrison and Paul McCartney – Electric and Acoustic Guitars*
>
> *Gary Brooker, Jools Holland, Chris Stainton, Billy Preston and Paul McCartney – Keyboards*
>
> *Dave Bronze and Klaus Voorman – Bass*
>
> *Ringo Starr, Jim Keltner, Jim Capaldi and Henry Spinetti – Drums*
>
> *Ray Cooper, Emil Richards and Jim Capaldi – Percussion*
>
> *Jim Horn – Tenor Saxophone*
>
> *Tom Scott – Alto Saxophone*
>
> *Katie Kissoon, Tessa Niles and Sam Brown – Backing Vocals*
>
> *Anoushka Shankar – Sitar*

With Eric and Jeff Lynne as musical directors, the band began to tackle the task of re-creating 26 of George's best-loved songs. There were times during the rehearsals when we all felt a deep connection to George through the power of his music. Playing together was an opportunity for us to pay our respects to him and to grieve for the man we loved in a way that visiting a grave could never do. Throughout our time at Asylum Studios various musicians came to augment the basic line-up. Ringo Starr joined us towards the end of rehearsals. He bounced in looking fabulously youthful and entertained us with his laconic humour. During a break one afternoon, Ringo turned to Eric and asked in his still broad Scouse accent, 'Hey Eric, what's that on your guitar?' Ringo pointed to the maker's name inscribed on the head of Eric's guitar.

'Erm, that's a Gibson Les Paul,' replied Eric.

'Oh, we could'a done with that in The Beatles,' said Ringo dryly.

Puzzled, Eric replied, 'But you had Les Paul guitars in The Beatles.'

'No you don't understand,' said Ringo, 'I mean what it says there, we could'a done with less Paul.'

The Concert for George took place on 29 November 2002. The Royal Albert Hall had been decorated for the occasion. Above the stage, draped with a backdrop of rich orange and gold, hung a black and white photograph of George as a young man. The smell of incense drifted lightly through the gilded auditorium and the red velvet seats cast a deep warm glow. George had touched my life through his friendship and enduring music, and this celebration was his gift to all of us who had known him. George's presence was felt everywhere that night: in his songs, in the beaming faces of the audience and in the way we all felt a connection to one another. This being a celebration of George's life there would of course be humour, and a hilarious performance by the Monty Python troupe with special guests Tom Hanks and Terry Gilliam was perfect. Their rousing version of *The Lumberjack Song* might have been considered inappropriate by some for a memorial concert; who but Monty Python, complete with bare bums, could delight a crowd so irreverently? George would have loved it.

The concert also featured moving performances from George's long-time friends, Ravi Shankar and his daughter Anoushka, Joe Brown, Tom Petty and The Heartbreakers, Jools Holland and

Sam Brown. The band steamed through one classic song to another. On *For You Blue*, Paul McCartney sang the lead with Ringo Starr on drums. It was the first time since The Beatles broke up that Ringo and Paul had made music together on the same stage. George's son Dhani, the image of his father, performed on every song with us. It would be hard to name a favourite song that night, but Billy Preston singing *My Sweet Lord* came pretty close. Billy's deeply soulful voice and spiritual Hammond playing touched everyone, bringing the audience to its feet. From the acoustic guitars in the intro and the much-loved slide guitar, to the chorus of voices blending Hallelujahs with Hare Krishna and Vedic prayer, *My Sweet Lord* is one of George Harrison's finest.

As the performers assembled on stage at the closing of the show, Joe Brown picked up a ukulele and began to strum *I'll See You in My Dreams*. It was a poignant moment, as everyone there knew of George's love for the humble instrument. A fitting tribute to our departed friend, like gently falling rain thousands of orange and yellow rose petals descended from the domed ceiling of the Albert Hall, while the soft lights caught reflections of tear-stained faces. Using music, humour and spirituality we honoured George that night. For me, Olivia expressed it best, 'Everyone on that stage would agree that there was no one more lovable or mystical than George. He was as rare as lightning striking the same place twice; flashing into our lives with intensity, lighting them up with a million candlepower and returning to the ether all too soon.'

The Robbie Williams band flew to Copenhagen in early December to film a concert for Danish television. I'd always enjoyed the city of Copenhagen for its history and sense of style, and for its unusual number of good-looking inhabitants. In my opinion Denmark has more gorgeous people than anywhere else in Europe, with Milan perhaps running a close second. The band stayed at The Palace Hotel, a handsome old building in the heart of the city. A blanket of snow covered the ground and outside the front of the hotel there was an ice rink. On our day off, the sky outside being a brilliant blue, Robbie suggested that the band should all go ice skating, so bundled up warmly against the cold we assembled by the rink.

I was a tad reluctant to skate as I'm not at my most confident on the ice. Noticing me standing behind the barrier, Robbie wobbled over to me on his skates and linked his arm through mine.

'Come on, Tess. Don't worry, you and me'll stay together, 'cos I'm crap at this,' he said, his green eyes glinting in the sunlight.

'Oh no, really, it's OK Rob, you go on, I'm really bad, honestly,' I replied.

'No, I won't hear of it. I'm the boss and you must do as I say,' Robbie joked as he pulled me away from the security of the barrier and out on to the ice.

'Oooh, look at us all Torville and Dean,' he laughed.

Nervously we began to move forward together while other skaters flew past. As we neared the middle of the rink, Robbie suddenly let go of my arm and with a dramatic flourish pushed himself forward and skated off like an Olympic champion. Stranded and wobbling on the ice it only took me a moment to realise the joke. As he gathered speed Robbie turned back and flashed me his most dazzling smile shouting 'Love you Tess'.

At home in Hadley Wood life revolved around preparations for the school holidays. I immersed myself in the twins' school activities, loving every minute. It felt good to be involved with normal family life after such a busy and emotionally taxing year. I made cupcakes and manned a stall at the Christmas bazaar, and the sound of the children singing carols in their first Nativity play had me in tears and bursting with unabashed pride. It was going to be hard spending Christmas without Molly, so every possible effort was put into making it a holiday to remember.

In February the Robbie Williams band embarked on a television promotional tour in the United States. When he signed his record-breaking contract, part of Robbie's agreement was that EMI would break him in the States; he had cracked almost every other territory but there. The band performed on *Good Morning America* and *The Carson Daly Show*, but despite great efforts the American public just didn't get Robbie Williams. They hadn't a clue who Take That were, and had no history with what they saw as some crazy Brit.

In London a studio date with Seal had me reconnect with my old friend Trevor Horn. Trevor had achieved huge success with Seal and was responsible for producing hits such as *Crazy* and the Grammy-winning *Kiss from A Rose*. I sang on *Get It Together* for his new album, *Seal IV*. Seal was not in the studio with us, having already recorded his vocals. As is often the case, just the sound engineer, the producer and I worked on the vocals.

Out of the four hit albums I worked on with Tina Turner, she was present in the studio for only one of them. During the recording of *Simply the Best* Tina and I had a deep and meaningful conversation.

'Personally I like to wait until I come outta the bath and then I attack 'em with a razor blade,' said Tina, slicing the air with her hands. 'You know, get 'em when they're warm.'

The recording engineer looked up from his desk unable to grasp what was going on.

'Really, you prefer to use a blade?' I questioned. 'But doesn't that hurt?'

Tina's famous mane bobbed up and down as she spoke.

'Ha! You better believe it's painful but it's all good in the long run. You don't want 'em comin' back.'

'Hmm... interesting,' I said, 'but don't you have someone that could do it for you?'

'Uh uh honey, some jobs you just gotta get in there and do yaself.'

For a woman that had spent a lifetime in heels I felt inclined to believe that when it came to bunions, Tina knew what she was talking about.

In August Eduardo and I jetted off with Kris, Alessia, Mikaela and Fallon to Egypt for a two-week holiday. This was to be our last hurrah before rehearsals began for the Robbie Williams European Tour and a bijou gig in the grounds of an old country house called Knebworth.

In 2003 the world reeled at the news that the government of Saddam Hussein had been overthrown by American forces. In the UK, with footie never far from the headlines, Chelsea FC was bought by Russian billionaire Roman Abramovitch. Beyoncé was at the top of the charts with *Crazy in Love* and my precious friend Pepi Lemer was in love. On 14 June she married her lifelong friend, television producer Paul Knight. The wedding, a glittering affair attended by family and friends, was held at London's famous Claridge's Hotel. My girls were bridesmaids, and the bride was a vision in peach. Pepi had gone through difficult times as a single parent struggling to provide for her girls Gabi and Dani, and the constant challenges of trying to sustain a career in jazz. I was beyond thrilled that my dearest friend, my closest confidante, my schwester, had at last found happiness. After a sumptuous feast and a modicum of alcohol I spoke about my bestest friend in the world. Pepi was radiant, her joy permeating among friends and family alike; she has always drawn people to her with her unique personality and keen interest in others. And, of course, with Pepi there was music; whether at an informal get-together or a big family occasion there would always be great music. It's her gift that she gives freely. I couldn't love her more.

After the wedding, rehearsals began in earnest for the Robbie Williams summer stadium tour of Europe aka Weekends of Mass Destruction. Robbie's career had now officially entered hyper-space and become an unstoppable force. This was to be his finest moment and biggest tour to date: 21 shows in front of 1.2 million people across Europe.

The band rehearsed on one of the huge sound stages at Elstree Film Studios. Robbie's set, lighting, elaborate special effects, sound and choreography were all raising the bar for stadium shows. The band also had a new member, Max Beesley, a multi-talented musician who was also in demand as an actor. The sandy-haired Mancunian had been friends with Robbie since the Take That days. In addition to Max, Robbie brought in six fabulous dancers to augment the line-up. Conspicuously missing from the band was musical director, co-writer and producer of many of Robbie's hits, Guy Chambers, who had been responsible

The Robbie Williams entourage and liveried RW plane, 2002.

for bringing Katie Kissoon and me into the Williams fold. He and Robbie had subsequently been involved in an acrimonious split. The Chambers and Williams partnership was legendary in music circles; they were likened to Lennon and McCartney for their ability to produce hit after hit. When working with the band Guy had been an exacting task master and perfectionist. His working relationship with Robbie was prolific and intense, but as is the case with many partnerships, not always plain sailing, and due to differences the two decided to end their relationship.

I missed the musical discipline that Guy brought to the proceedings, but the Robbie Williams train was ready to roll on without him. OK, we no longer travelled by train and there would be no gruelling bus journeys on this tour; Robbie and the band now travelled in a private plane complete with RW livery. There were also ten crew buses and 54 trucks, hauling luggage, pyrotechnics, sound equipment, catering supplies and more across Europe. The weeks of intense rehearsals came to a close with Robbie showing up for the last few days. It amazed me how he could be so damn good with so little practice. Many performers used rehearsal time to strengthen their voices and build up show stamina, but not Robbie; he seemed fit, fully prepared and hungry to get his game on.

Our first two warm-up shows were in Edinburgh at Murrayfield Stadium. The opening of the concert was signalled by a World War II air raid siren. Above the centre of the stage Robbie hung upside-down, Houdini-like, from a chain and was slowly lowered on to the stage. Upon touchdown the band exploded into the opening number, *Let Me Entertain You*, as the giant video screens magnified Robbie's every gesture. With the force of a locomotive Robbie powered through the set of old and new numbers, relentlessly selling his unique brand of high-octane showmanship; he never failed to astound even the musicians on stage, who had watched him perform over a period of years. For me, Robbie's extraordinary talent will always be a force of nature.

Our 'blended' Mondlane family: Kristofer, Tessa, Eduardo Jr, Fallon, Alessia and Mikaela, 2001.

Eduardo and I had worked out a plan to be able to see each other on the breaks between touring and, where possible, during the tour. Living this way was taking its toll on both of us and the strain was beginning to show. Touring had again become the nature of my work, but I knew deep down that it couldn't go on forever. The twins needed me more and more, and despite working hard at keeping my relationship with Eduardo fresh, the time and distance between us was becoming a problem. The feeling was all too familiar to me and I couldn't allow myself to repeat the mistakes of the past.

Over the years Eduardo and I had discussed making changes that would involve moving the family to South Africa. His business was there and was suffering due to the fact that he spent so much time in England. While my parents were alive the idea of moving had been shelved as I couldn't envisage living away from them, but things had changed and it was time to rethink. But could I seriously contemplate giving up the career I had worked so hard to establish? Could I reinvent myself in another country, without friends or family? It all seemed a step too far, but at the end of each tour it was becoming harder for Eduardo and me to adjust back into our relationship; the dynamics between us were shifting and we were no longer communicating. We bickered with each other, resentment simmering just below the surface. We had changed, and our lives were no longer moving in the same direction. I was well versed in the dangers of spending time apart. I'd been there before and could see that issues of trust and jealousy had begun to raise their ugly heads. Did I really need more proof that this relationship was heading downhill fast? In spite of our love for each other, the life Eduardo and I had built was in danger of falling apart.

Tessa and Katie Kissoon on the Robbie Williams Tour, 2002.

The Weekends of Mass Destruction tour rolled on successfully throughout Europe, performing to hundreds of thousands of people. Days were spent travelling, rehearsing, sightseeing when we could – and of course shopping. My partner in crime Katie Kissoon and I were shoppers of note. She and I were perfectly attuned when it came to all things retail. Fuelled by the occasional cappuccino, Katie and I could go for hours, relentless in our quest to shop the world. We even had intuitive built-in homing devices so that in any store, anywhere on the planet, we could always find each other. Our purchases became the stuff of legend. We were known for buying cutlery in New York, curtains in Paris, paintings in Rio and a carriage clock in Vienna. On one occasion Katie was held for some time at Heathrow airport on suspicion of smuggling narcotics, but after an official inspection the suspicious white substance carried back from a visit to the Dead Sea was found to be a lump of salt.

Tessa and Katie Kissoon taking a break while Robbie performs Mr Bojangles on the Weekends of Mass Destruction Tour, 2003.

Over the first three days of August the band prepared to perform three shows at Knebworth, the country park where I had performed with Eric Clapton, Elton John and Mark Knopfler back in 1990. The gigs were filmed for release on DVD. A record-breaking 375,000 tickets were sold in less than eight hours for the three shows and set a world attendance record for a run of shows by a single artist. There was no doubt that my boss, Robbie Williams, was on fire. The DVD, entitled *What We Did Last Summer*, went platinum seven times in the UK.

Sitting in a restaurant, eating pizza with my girls while on a break between tours, I received a call from one of Robbie's managers.

'Hi Tess, it's Tim. How are you?'

'All good thanks, Tim. To what do I owe this pleasure?'

'Well, I'm really carrying a message from Robbie.'

'Ooh I'm intrigued.'

*Preparing for the show on the Robbie Williams
Weekends of Mass Destruction Tour, 2003.*

'As a thank you for taking part in the Knebworth shows, he'd like to give you a gift.'

'Really, that's very generous of him.'

Tim proceeded to tell me that Robbie wanted to give each band member a cash gift. With mozzarella and tomato dripping from my gaping mouth, I sat back in my seat in a state of shock. The gift was a large enough sum to keep me happily in pizza for the rest of my life.

After a short break the Robbie Williams tour resumed in October. Renamed for this leg The Cock of Justice Tour, the band reconvened in Portugal and we rocked our way through Spain, France, Italy, Switzerland, Poland, the Czech Republic, Hungary, Russia, Finland and finally Norway. It was quite strange to be bathed in the adulation of thousands of screaming fans in foreign cities one week and doing the school run in my slippers the next.

Talk about living a double life! For the final leg of the tour the band travelled to New Zealand and Australia where Robbie continued to wow his audiences, and came to a close in Sydney. The band celebrated in true rock 'n' roll style, somehow sensing that this time together would never come again. Our intense year of touring had been a resounding success. I'd loved every minute in the Robbie Williams band, forming friendships with extraordinary people and making music with exceptional musicians. I felt privileged to have got to know and love Robbie, but knew it was time to take a hard look at my personal life and make some decisions, decisions that would not come easily. After the long flight back from Australia the band said their emotional farewells to one another in the arrivals hall at Heathrow airport.

My heart was quietly breaking, as I knew this tour would be remembered as my last.

Tessa, Robbie Williams and Katie Kissoon singing the a cappella introduction to Rock DJ, 2003

CHAPTER TEN

Backing the future

As always after a tour ended, I felt a sense of loss; this time more than ever, perhaps because I knew that life was forcing me to confront the changes that were necessary. People who had been an integral part of my existence on the road for months at a time were no longer there. Katie, Claire and Yolanda were no longer in their rooms just down the hotel corridor from mine. Friends who had become like family to me were moving on with their lives, as I needed to.

In a way, being on the road had been like living in a virtual world, where for the most part people who shared the adrenalin-fuelled, surreal experience of performing to adoring masses every night were good-humoured, upbeat and carefree. In the real world, where my bathroom needed cleaning and children needed to be fed, I no longer had a tour manager telling me what time I should be ready for the limo to pick me up, or what party I would be attending. One minute a rock chick, the next a housewife and mother who was facing up to the fact that her relationship was in trouble.

It was proving harder and harder to shield the children from arguments. The resentment that had been building up over several years was now undeniable. One day, after an almighty showdown, Eduardo and I threw every gripe, grievance, frustration and accusation we had into the pot, and at that painful point we also threw in the towel. Both of us had grown tired of the fights that were beginning to impact on everyone in the family, and with the heaviest of hearts we decided to split up. Neither of us knew if time apart would help us make sense of things. We didn't even know if our relationship was salvageable, and as Eduardo flew down to Mozambique I found sanctuary, as always, in the recording studio.

With my heart in pieces, I focused on working with Robbie on his sixth studio album, *Intensive Care*, and embarked on presenting a six-part series for BBC Radio 4. The series involved teaching music to young children through songs and storytelling. This was a real departure for me and the perfect time to throw myself into a new challenge. Since they were born I'd sung to my girls at every possible opportunity, so to reach a broader audience of children was wonderful.

The studio had always been my first love, and upon hearing that I'd been booked on a session with my favourite actor, Kevin Spacey, my spirits lifted. Kevin was co-writing, directing and co-producing *Beyond the Sea*, a biographical film based on the life of singer/actor Bobby Darin. Kevin was lovely – a total gentleman and a great singer. He explained that the scene in the film we were working on was set in a nightclub, where character Bobby Darin is singing a protest song called *Simple Song of Freedom.* Carol Kenyon, Lance Ellington, Kevin Spacey and I dubbed the voices of the gospel choir appearing in the scene behind Bobby. We had so much fun together. Kevin was utterly charming. It's always a relief when masters of their craft turn out to be nice people too.

Shortly after, *Beyond the Sea* producer Trevor Horn hired me for another film session. Trevor was working on the theme song for the Hollywood film *King Arthur*, starring Keira Knightley and Clive Owens. 2003 turned out to be a bumper year for working on films when shortly after I sang on the opening title sequence for *Alfie*, a remake of the 60s classic starring the delectable Jude Law.

Sessions were keeping me busy, but I was struggling in coming to terms with living apart from Eduardo. He had been my world for so long. He'd supported my career and I his. We had built a family and had weathered some extraordinarily difficult times together. His divorce from first wife, Paola, had been a long and protracted process but we'd all worked hard at blending the two families together. After 14 years, Eduardo and I shared a deep and unconditional love for all our children. I missed him.

My friend Katie and I had been a partnership since we'd first sung on a Gloria Gaynor session 18 years earlier. Katie and I had never argued in all the time we had known each other; our relationship was entirely uncomplicated, both on and off stage. On *The Rat Pack* tribute album by Irish boy band Westlife, the two of us worked a little nostalgic magic on songs made famous by Frank Sinatra and Nat King Cole. Katie and I sang on *That's Life*, backed by a 60-piece orchestra. The experience of singing with an orchestra of that size is indescribable; the emotion and sheer power of so many musicians playing together is awe inspiring.

Eduardo and I agreed that we needed to see a counsellor to help us try to salvage our battered relationship. The first session was incredibly painful as we both remained angry and accusatory. Neither of us wanted to listen to the other's point of view and we left the counsellor's office with the opinion that the process probably wasn't going to work. We went for coffee.

'What did you think about what happened in there?' I asked.

Eduardo looked broken as he stared down at his cup. 'I don't really know, we both said some hurtful things.'

A cheery waiter asked if everything was OK.

I wanted to scream that no, actually, everything was not OK.

'It's sort of hard to see past what was said right now,' said Eduardo.

'Yeah it is hard... but it needed to be done,' I said, putting on my coat. 'I'll see you soon.'

The truth stung and neither of us wanted to take responsibility for it. Despite the anger we both knew there was a process to follow, with no guarantees or quick fixes. It hurt.

Music had never failed to heal my pain. Simply to wake up each day knowing that I'd be making music held wonder for me. During this raw emotional time, work became a refuge and solace, and the chance to perform with old friends Duran Duran a welcome distraction. Earlier in the year I'd worked on *Astronaut*, my fifth album with the band, in which we had travelled three decades of pop together. The boys and I flew out to Berlin to perform a series of promotional gigs for the new album.

Duran Duran backstage, (L to R) Roger Taylor, Dom Brown, John Taylor, Tessa, Simon Le Bon, Nick Rhodes and Andy Hamilton, 2004.

Meanwhile, in London Trevor Horn was busy putting together a band to perform at a huge concert at Wembley Arena to celebrate his own illustrious 25-year career in British pop. I was asked to be part of the group that would sing back-up vocals for the artists appearing on the show. The band was made up of the best of British session musicians, all of them having had a long association with Trevor.

Among the artists performing that night, all of whom had had their hits produced by the maestro of pop, were Lisa Stansfield, The Pet Shop Boys, Yes, Grace Jones, Dollar, Propaganda, ABC, Frankie Goes to Hollywood, Tatu, Seal and Simple Minds. Proceeds from the concert were to go to The Prince's Trust Organisation. On the night of the concert, before the show began, Trevor and the musicians gathered at a small reception backstage.

Tessa and Prince Charles exchanging views at the Produced by Trevor Horn concert for The Prince's Trust, 2004.

Prince Charles and his soon-to-be wife Camilla Parker Bowles graciously greeted the gathering. As I stood on the periphery I suddenly felt a firm hand in the small of my back.

'This way Mrs, you're coming with me,' said Trevor's wife Jill Sinclair as she gently pushed me towards the group gathered around Prince Charles. When we reached the front of the group Jill turned to the Prince and announced, 'Your Royal Highness, may I present Tessa Niles. She is one of the vocalists in this evening's show and a much-valued member of Trevor's team.'

Both Charles and Camilla shook my hand and greeted me as I tentatively dropped a curtsey. They were warm and at ease as we talked about the history of the Prince's Duchy food products, and the future of organic farming in Britain. I'm grateful to Jill, who knew that a backing singer sometimes needs a shove to the fore.

With the aid of a counsellor and a real and present fear of losing all that we valued, after much soul searching Eduardo and

I decided that there were more good things in our relationship than bad, and that we would fight to rebuild our love for each other. We both knew this would take time, patience and willingness on both sides to make changes. There were things I didn't really want to address about my life, things that were challenging and removed me from my comfort zone. I would have to consider making sacrifices. I had always been a singer and performer, yes, but did my profession define me as a person? If you took that away, was I any less me? Was it more important to have a successful family life or a successful career? And was it possible to have both?

This was a pivotal moment and the time had come to take a long hard look at the future. Without doubt Eduardo and I both needed to make changes; we could no longer carry on with me touring and him away on business for weeks at a time. I knew that this was absolutely not the way I wanted to bring up my children, which made the decision-making process easier. Children are little for such a short time and I was unwilling to miss any more of their growing years. Home was where I wanted to be, and home could be anywhere in the world as long as the family were together. I was 44 years old and had achieved many of the goals I'd set for myself. I was successful and financially independent, but deep down I knew that what was needed was a leap of faith on my part. How could I expect to see change if I myself was not prepared to make changes? Since there were few opportunities for Eduardo's business to grow in England, he needed to be in southern Africa.

I'd always known that if you search long enough for the answers you seek, they will come. The answers did come, but they made me feel vulnerable, something I had protected myself against all my life. Since I'd been a young girl, standing in the studio behind a microphone and layering my voice on to tape had been the safest environment I knew. The studio had always been my sanctuary, a place where I could seclude myself from the rest of the world; a place of creativity and exploration – my church, you might say.

Trevor Horn and I had worked together for many years and being part of his creative team was something I truly valued. During the months of considering my future, working in the studio with Trevor was, as always, challenging but therapeutic. On one session I was called upon to be the unofficial third member of Russian pseudo-lesbian duo Tatu, on their CD *Dangerous and Moving*. On another occasion I was required to change vocal gender and sing male-sounding backing vocals for Enrique Iglesias. For my fourth album with The Pet Shop Boys I layered multi-tracks of voices for the single *I'm with Stupid*.

Following the sessions with Trevor I jumped at an opportunity to teach a master class on session singing to a group of aspiring singers at the Brighton Institute of Modern Music. I prepared well for the class and was surprised at how great it felt to talk in depth about the career I loved. After about an hour I introduced a Q and A session. During the talk I had stressed the importance of building one's reputation as a singer in the music industry, so was utterly baffled when a rather vacant-looking girl in the third row asked, 'Have you ever slept with anyone famous?'

After doing my best to provide an overview of the skills necessary for my job, I was floored. It was as if this girl had no reference point from which to comprehend the job I had worked at my whole life. Initially I was affronted by her cavalier attitude to my hard-earned achievements, and then took a minute to look the audience over. I saw that the average age of the students was around 18 or 19 years old; at their age, could I really expect them to understand where I was coming from? Knowing my answer would no doubt disappoint, I replied in true Mae West fashion, 'My dears, if I had, I would no longer be here to tell the tale.'

Life for Eduardo and me was about to transform. There was no way we could make small changes to the way we lived, we had to shake things up completely. Eduardo needed to become the main breadwinner of the family and I needed to take on the supporting role: a question of life imitating art. We made the decision to leave England and build a new life for ourselves in South Africa. It was obvious that we could not both travel anymore, I now knew with clarity that I needed to give up my career to support Eduardo in his. I believed Eduardo had the capacity to do great things if he was given the opportunity. We had in fact thought for some years about making this move, when the time was right. Alessia, now 14, had moved to Rome with her mother, and Kristofer, who was 19, was at university in the States. It had never seemed the right time before; there had always been my career to consider, and knowing how much it meant to me Eduardo would never have asked me to give it up. But now we both knew this was the right thing to do for all of us. Family was the most important thing in my life, and the reason behind the difficult decisions I was now making.

There were also practical concerns, of course. Eduardo and I knew a level of risk would be involved in moving to a country with a high crime rate. At times, the magnitude of the decisions threatened to overwhelm me; could I really leave the life I knew and loved for the unknown? Could I leave everything that was familiar, and my family and friends? These were questions that would destabilise me over the coming months, doubts that threatened at times to sabotage my resolve. In spite of them, I knew in my heart that I needed to make this leap of faith.

The first step in implementing the plan was to sell the house, a daunting prospect in a market that for five years had seen unstoppable price rises, but was now showing signs of faltering. With the house price established, it went on the market and the waiting game began. I told few people of our plan to move to South Africa and when I received a call from Robbie Williams to work with him, realised that this would be for the last time.

Live 8 was held in Hyde Park, London, with another ten concerts taking place – often simultaneously – around the world. These shows were part of the Global Call for Action against Poverty, planned to coincide with the 20th anniversary of the 1985 Live Aid concert. More than 1,000 musicians were to participate in the shows, which were timed to precede the G8 summit in Scotland.

Once again, the world's greatest pop music stars turned out to show their support. Among the artists performing were Pink Floyd, Madonna, Coldplay, Mariah Carey, U2, Youssou N'Dour and Paul McCartney. On the day of the Hyde Park concert, Kristofer and Alessia accompanied their seven-year-old sisters. I was petrified they'd lose each other in the massive crowds and suggested that they somehow tie themselves together, an idea that was swiftly vetoed by the teens. Hyde Park heaved with people who'd come from far and wide to lend their support to the fight against poverty. Backstage the vibe was electric as performers fraternised with each other from their portakabin dressing rooms. That day there were more celebrities, stars, game changers and attention-seekers per square metre than I had ever seen. Mr and Mrs Beckham were hanging out with Elton John; Bob Geldof was working like a pro backstage, introducing Snoop Dog to Kofi Anan and Brad Pitt to Bill Gates. Pop royalty and the world's movers and shakers were crammed into a cordoned-off section of London parkland which, for once, was not dampened by the British weather.

As always, Robbie was incredible, evoking the spirit of the late, great Freddie Mercury when he sang *We Will Rock You*. During the song *Angels*, Robbie's best-loved ballad, the crowd sang along. With the formidable sound of this 200,000-strong choir and the lights of London across the park, I was overcome by the power and emotion of the moment. Robbie held the audience in the palm of his hand and I knew from the heaviness I felt in my chest that this would be the last time I'd perform at such an event. The decision to leave all that I had ever known weighed heavily on me at that moment as I realised that this would soon become my past. I left a piece of me behind forever on stage that night as I sang through my tears.

The waiting was interminable. The housing market had ground to a halt and keeping Number Eight in pristine condition with two children bent on claiming every tidy space was a challenge. Then, out of nowhere, a charming and mercifully financially un-encumbered couple saved the day and made a successful bid for the house. The big changes in our lives were now really happening, we were past the point of no return. With a new beginning beckoning I decided to sell most of the things inside the house;

I quite relished the idea of acquiring new stuff in South Africa, so organised what Americans would call a yard sale. With price stickers on everything that wasn't coming with us, I sat back and watched as our belongings dwindled away to just a bed, clothes and art works.

Eduardo had flown to South Africa on a reconnaissance mission to look for a place to live and check out schools for the twins. Our major concern was safety. In Johannesburg gated communities that offer security in pleasant surroundings are plentiful. Eduardo chose a house to let on a golf estate in the northern part of Johannesburg. In the perfectly groomed grounds were 1,400 houses, sports facilities and club houses; a slice of suburban heaven, albeit behind state-of-the-art security walls. It was a lifestyle that would take some getting used to.

For the two months we had left in England, the family moved out of the house and into a small bungalow. As I focused on our new life, the fear that had originally gripped me began to dissipate. The bungalow reminded me of my grandparents' place at Frinton-on-Sea: their tidy bungalow with its potted plants, crocheted toilet roll holders and candlewick bedspreads. The feeling of having few belongings was not unpleasant. With the containers packed and ready to sail to Durban, I finally allowed myself a minute to acknowledge that this was the end of an era.

There was never a time when I didn't feel excited at going to work, but as I set off on a freezing October day for what was to be my final recording session my mood was reflective. As the taxi headed out towards Shepherds Bush the cockney driver shouted back to me, 'Ere love, that place on the right there is Nigella's old house. You know, the posh bird that makes a fortune doin' the cookin?' Rows of Victorian terraced houses flashed by, and through the window I observed the familiar sights and sounds of London. Noteworthy, as if I were seeing them for the first time: a bus popping with colour against the grey leafless sky, and people hunched over against the cold. The taxi pulled up outside the studio. Katie was waiting for me in the lobby where we hugged in silence.

The old life was losing its hold as thoughts of the new gathered speed. Setting up on that final session, the producer's voice came through the headphones, asking if the sound was OK and was there was anything more I needed. Thinking hard, I replied, 'No, nothing at all thanks, I've had all the run-throughs I could ever need. I'm so ready.'

My hearts, (L to R) Mikaela, Fallon, Kristofer and Alessia, 2012.

Photo: Annabel Newell.

About the author

If you were listening to music during the 1980s and 1990s then chances are that Tessa Niles performed live with some of your favourite artists and sang on your most loved tracks. Her first big break came in 1983 when Sting asked her to join The Police on the Synchronicity World Tour. Niles went on to perform with David Bowie at the legendary Live Aid concert and sang on Bowie and Jagger's hit *Dancing in the Streets*.

She then joined Eric Clapton's band and collaborated on the first of MTV's *Unplugged* series which spawned the classic versions of *Layla* and *Tears in Heaven*. Producer Trevor Horn and Niles worked on many projects together including The Pet Shop Boys, ABC, Grace Jones, Frankie Goes to Hollywood, Tatu and Seal.

She worked on four albums with Tina Turner and on the worldwide hits *What's Love Got To Do With It?* and *Simply The Best.* Niles recorded with Duran Duran on their hits *Come Undone* and *Notorious.* She sang on the soundtrack to the films *Love Actually, Four Weddings and a Funeral* and *Bridget Jones's Diary.*

Throughout the last three decades Tessa Niles has performed with some of the most iconic artists in music: George Harrison, Annie Lennox, Tears For Fears, The Pet Shop Boys, The Rolling Stones, Paul McCartney, Elton John, Kylie Minogue and Robbie Williams to name a few.

Testimonials

"I can neither confirm nor deny that I've contemplated sleeping with Tessa Niles' talent on several occasions."

- Robbie Williams

"Tessa Niles has done what so many fans only dreamed of: sing with the stars. Throughout Backtrack I was enchanted, delighted and moved to hear her vivid true story of the backing singer extraordinaire relaying a singularly unique point of view of someone who was right there when music history was made. A riveting read."

- Jonathan G Shaw:
music producer, lecturer and author of
'The South African Music Business'

"Tessa went on to be one of the busiest and certainly in my view the best session singer of her generation."

- Trevor Horn:
Brit and Grammy Award winning pop music producer for ABC,
Tina Turner, Seal, The Pet Shop Boys, Grace Jones, Paul McCartney,
Annie Lennox, Robbie Williams.

"I think there is a really special art in a vocalist being able to sit and blend in any track of any style with any singer whilst retaining something so inherently magical that it stands out without intruding on the lead vocal. For me Tessa Niles is the ultimate backing singer not only because she does it with grace and excellence but because her knowledge of harmony is second to none and she always brings so much joy with her wherever she goes. I fall in love with voices rarely but I fell in love with hers the moment we did our first session and have been that way ever since"

- Steve Anderson:
Producer/Musical Director for Kylie, Leona Lewis and Delta Goodrem

"Throughout my career in music, there have been a select few people who have been omnipresent. Tessa Niles is amongst them. The fact that she has been one of the worlds leading session singers and artists for many years is testament to her talent, her professionalism and her ability to adapt to so many aspects of performance and genres.

I have been fortunate enough to work with Tessa in a variety of situations, including studios, concert halls, theatres and stadiums, both as a soloist and backing vocalist. Her dedication, hard work and constant study are qualities that I have always admired and learnt from. Her presence, on and off stage, brings something special to every musical occasion, making it no surprise that she has worked with the greatest artists in the World throughout her career."

- Steve Sidwell:
Grammy Award winning orchestrator, composer,
musician and musical director for The Voice.

"Tessa Niles is one of the finest singers I have ever had the pleasure of working with. Together we recorded and toured extensively with the Eric Clapton Band. Those adventures alone including the making of Clapton's iconic "MTV Unplugged" album and George Harrison's final tour in Japan make BACKTRACK a compelling read. Experience this wonderful journey and get ready to hear the amazing stories behind the voice behind the stars brilliantly told by Tessa Niles!"

- Nathan East:
Grammy nominated writer and producer and considered
one of the most recorded bass players in the history of music.